THE
I-HATE-TOURISTS
GUIDEBOOK

The totally, utterly and completely unabridged
guide to the confusion, bedevilment, deception,
delusion, and downright annoyance of foreign
visitors to these shores.

THE
I-HATE-
TOURISTS
GUIDEBOOK

EDITOR
Geoffrey Atkinson

Illustrated by Borin Van Loon

Published by
The Britons Against Tourism Association
in association with
GRAFTON BOOKS
A Division of the Collins Publishing Group

LONDON GLASGOW
TORONTO SYDNEY AUCKLAND

Grafton Books
A Division of the Collins Publishing Group
8 Grafton Street, London W1X 3LA

A Grafton Paperback Original 1988

ISBN 0-586-07137-7

Printed and bound in Great Britain

Set in Century Schoolbook

This book is dedicated to the foreign visitor to Britain, without whom . . . the place would be a lot better

CONTENTS

PREFACE

There was a time when you could choose whether or not to meet other nationals simply by going abroad or staying at home. Nowadays alas the luxury has been denied us by the hordes of foreign tourists swamping our shores each year. It seems that no longer are we safe from foreign intrusion if we stay at home. Indeed, not even the maxim that an Englishman's home is his castle is preserved. Nowadays his castle, if he has one, is very likely to be open to the public and overrun by an unwanted mass of foreign trippers. This volume is for all those whose lives are miserably ruined by this overseas onslaught.

BRITONS

AGAINST

TOURISM

ASSOCIATION

A MESSAGE FROM THE LIFE PRESIDENT OF BATA

BATA was formed in 1968 because of growing public pressure to do something about the increasing number of foreigners visiting our shores each year. Its central principle was quite simple; to get all the foreign muck out of our country.

Since then the association has not ceased in its efforts to fight tourism in our country. Just look at some of the great things we at BATA propose to introduce:

● The presentation of a complimentary sachet of honest British dog muck to all foreign guests visiting British shores.

● A dead cockroach in every hotel room booked by a foreign national.

● A 'Stick To Your Own Grot Hole, You Poxy Gits' campaign to be launched in all major European countries.

● A new law under which foreign visitors will be deported from Britain as soon as they have cleared customs and surrendered their travellers' cheques.

BATA is the only organization in Britain to actively campaign for the cessation of all foreign tourism to Britain. And we have pledged not to stop until we have achieved a totally touristless society in Great Britain.

BATA is pleased to offer its support to this book. Now at last the ordinary man-in-the-street-trying-to-get-past-hordes-of-bloody-tourists has a text to show him how to cope!

Let's hope that with books like this about, Johnny scumbags foreigner will get the message once and for all and stay at home in his own poky hovel.

I'm proud to say I hate tourists.

And I'm proud that this book says it too.

Tom Flemmings

Major General Tom Flemmings
'Buttercups'
Esher

BRITONS AGAINST TOURISM ASSOCIATION

MESSAGE TO ALL MEMBERS

'Tolerance is a great British virtue
— let's not waste it on a pack of bloody foreigners.'

1

INTRODUCTION

INTRODUCTION

You can't get tickets at Stratford because they've all gone to foreigners. You have to wait two hours to be served in Harrods because the American in front of you wants to buy six cashmere sweaters and the assistant can't leave him unattended for two seconds, and this even though you only want a pair of socks and have got the correct change. You have to play hopscotch down Horseguards Parade just to avoid the great mass of foreign sightseers clogging the pavement. These are the rewards that our blossoming tourist trade has brought us. And it is not just for a season, a few short summer months when the streets of London are paved with froggies and the tourist sights of Britain filled with the detritus from abroad. Now they come on the dot of 1 January and are with us till the clocks strike midnight on New Year's Eve. 'Britain in Bloom', 'Britain in Autumn', 'Summer Holidays', 'Winter Holidays', 'Late Season Breaks'. York, Canterbury, Edinburgh, Bath, Oxford.

Find a corner of Britain that the foreign tourist has still to discover and you can bet you won't have it to yourself for long. How we can still produce brochures with 'Discover The Delights of Britain' emblazoned across the top is surely a mystery, since there is now nothing left of Britain for the foreigner to discover! 'Discover the Bits of Britain that 70,000 of your Fellow Countrymen Have Discovered Before You' would be a more truthful slogan to use. 'Discover the One Bit of Britain that a Fat Family of Germans in a Mercedes Caravanette Haven't Yet Found' would be the more honest approach. Instead, though, we end up with another planeload of their compatriots discovering for the umpteenth time that discovery is the last thing to expect on a two-week air-conditioned coach tour of Britain.

BRITONS

AGAINST

TOURISM

ASSOCIATION

Standing Firm

Britons Against Tourism Association
Xenophobics Department
Churchill Annexe
Montgomery House
Cheltenham Spa
Gloucestershire
ENGLAND.

17

Get Lost!

BATA helps to fight the onslaught of foreign tourists to Britain. Help us to help you. Support BATA's "GET LOST" campaign. A campaign to get rid of the foreign tourist to these shores. Join BATA today. Before it's too late.

You get all this when you join **BATA**

◊ Anti-Tourist Kit

◊ Membership card ◊ BATA tie

◊ Associate Membership of the Monday Club ◊ BATA anti-tourist truncheon

◊ BATA limpet mine

◊ BATA round the clock protection

◊ BATA Newsletter and publication list ◊ Badge

◊ Discounts on all anti-tourist products

Your details
Name _____
Address _____
Age_____ Phone No. _____
Occupation _____

BATA is open to all people over 18 who hate foreign tourists. All applications are treated in strictest confidence.

 **THERE'S NONE BETTER THAN BATA**

2

HOW TO RECOGNIZE A FOREIGN TOURIST

Cut out and affix to window to prevent unwelcome intrusion by French visitors.

HOW TO RECOGNIZE A
FOREIGN TOURIST

The number of tourists on the street at any particular time is measured by the Foreign Tourist (or FT) index.

The FT index measures the proportion of foreigners walking the streets as a percentage of the total number of persons present.

FT Index

0	Normal
5	Minor foreign presence
10	Increased foreign presence
25	Large foreign presence
50	Extremely heavy foreign presence
75	Near takeover by foreigners
100	Complete takeover by foreigners
100+	ARGHHH!!!

For further details of the FT index and fresh information you should contact the British Telecom FT line which gives the daily FT reading for principal British cities and sites of interest.

British
TELECOM

FT-line

Find out the worst
blackspots.
Where are all the
foreign tourists?
What are the places
to avoid?

Dial HATELINE,
ask the operator
to connect you.

HOTEL

BUREAU
DE CHANGE

It is normally quite easy to spot a foreign tourist in the street. Where doubts persist the following abridged checklist should be employed.

Japanese

Diminutive, yellow-skinned, pinch-eyed nuisances with compulsive desire to photograph anything in their path. The average Japanese visitor is estimated to take a snap once every 5.8 seconds of their waking time when on holiday, and 10.2 seconds when asleep. The Japanese rarely make their own individual transport arrangements and are usually shifted around the country in large homogeneous groups by motor coach, stopping occasionally to allow the travelling photographers just enough time to get out and run off yet another roll of shots for the album before moving on to the next beauty spot. It has been estimated that over 75% of all Japanese tourists believe the entire continent of Europe comprises a series of neatly-bordered panoramic vistas, the product of a lifetime spent with eye glued firmly to view-finder .

American

Brash, loud, swanky, mawkishly-inclined troublemakers who have consistently failed to realize that the warm-hearted benevolence offered to English visitors in America is not necessarily reciprocated by their British counterparts when Americans come over here. The traditional view of the fat rich slob with a wallet full of mastercharge cards and a shopping list the length of a football field still holds good, but these days the style now includes a white flag, a steel trench helmet, and a near perpetual look of rabid fear: Libyan terrorists are thought to lurk on every corner. The irony that Americans were happy to stir things in the Med. content in the knowledge that 3000 miles of water cushioned them from the scene of any conflict seems strangely lost on the transatlantic visitor who is not interested in the politics of the affair, and only wants to return home safely, preferably not in a coffin with the stars and stripes draped over it. Europe is quite simply a dangerous place and the best way to see it is from the heavily tinted windows of a bullet-proof limo, or while dodging the gunfire on a shopping trip down Oxford Street.

Europeans

It had been intended to identify the particular national types visiting our shores and to pen individual portraits for each. Alas, though, with the coming of the Common Market the great mass of European tourists form a single generic species to which all national types conform. He or she will have impeccable English, a good knowledge of our country and customs, and will differ only in size, shape and form. Nordic types tend to be blonde, well attired, and bristling with good manners. The Germans will be physically similar but their manners will be less polished and they will exhibit a tendency to salute unnecessarily. Germans have a marked tendency to want to take things over (see Europe 1939–1945). If there is a place of interest to be seen then Germans will prepare for the visit as if it were a military campaign and will not be satisfied until they have taken over and 'conquered' the site. If the hotel residents' lounge has a television set then the Germans will control it. Sit next to a party of Germans in a restaurant and it is very likely that they will annexe your table, and very probably the one next to it.

The Austrians are a variant on the German type with similar habits but a tendency to salute even more. They will often salute stationary objects and will certainly raise a salute to the waitress when she brings their food. Austrians will march whenever possible and care should be taken when taking to the floor when Austrians are dancing. Unless they are specifically asked to break step while performing there is a very real risk of severe structural damage to the building occurring as well as the inevitable loss of life.

The Swiss is a further variant on this form with less saluting but more money. The Swiss are unique in being able to make you feel guilty about your *own* standard of English grammar when they speak to you.

The Italian male is small, dark, swarthy, and marked by overtight trousers and a packet of cigarettes clutched firmly in the hand because there's no room in his pockets. He has an obsessive need to wear sunglasses even on dark winter evenings. The Italian woman wears fur coats, especially in July, and shouts loudly at the Italian male, especially in restaurants.

The French tourist is similar in form but likely to have a contemptuous sneer on his face the way that only the French know how. French women, smaller than their Italian counterparts, can be seen scuttling round your local branch of Marks and Sparks, dressed in navy blue and clutching large armfuls of more navy blue clothes. Alone among visitors the French retain a steadfast and unbreakable refusal to speak anything but their mother tongue and will go to enormous lengths in their rejection of even the most basic of English words.

The Spanish and the Portuguese are similar to the Italians but can be readily distinguished by their tendency to wear ridiculously out-of-date shirts and flared trousers.

Australians

Australians are unique among nations in their habit of never taking a holiday of less than six months' duration. Not that you can blame them for staying away for so long when returning to Australia is such an unappealing prospect. Australians seem unabashed by the conventions of normal British protocol and will quite happily wander around the most holy of cathedrals in cut-down shorts and a T-shirt with 'Don't Come Near Me Cos I've Just Farted' printed across the back. If ever a nation lived up, or down, to its natural stereotype, then it is surely the Aussies. Aussie tourists tend to look similar to British tourists abroad only without the swollen red skin of the British holidaymaker.

New Zealanders

On first inspection quite similar to Australians. New Zealand tourists can be distinguished by the great abundance of Kiwi stickers, New Zealand badges and assorted NZ paraphernalia about their person. Crushed by mistaken identity for Australian for two centuries, the New Zealander exerts his nationality forcefully. Well, as forcefully as two rucksack stickers and a plethora of lapel badges allow.

Sri Lankans

Similar to other sub-Indianic races but notable for a propensity for removing their trousers in public and parading around Heathrow in their underpants, giving them more than a passing resemblance to a touring Ray Cooney theatre party.

Saudi Arabians, Omanis, Abu Dhabians and sundry other Arab groups

Distinguished by shifty eyes, sharp fingers, and a level of dental hygiene we wouldn't normally expect to find even in a goat over here in England. Generally carry £100,000 cash and a 'registered Marks and Spencer shoplifter' card in their back pockets. Arabs are notable for buying all the best seats at the opera, for taking up eight parking spaces with their special stretched Mercedes limos, and for pushing up the going rate for Shepherd Market hookers to a price the poor British businessman can't possibly afford.

Turks

Recognizable by a swarthy complexion and an appearance that is the spitting image of all London mini-cab drivers .

Moroccans/Algerians

Leather-skinned Mediterranean types with genetic predisposition towards crime. Never pre-offer your hand to an Algerian. You don't know if you will get it back.

Greeks

Notable for their Olympic Airlines travel bag with a name like Thoppodoppoloppolis on the tag and a suit that looks as if it has just been washed in taramasalata. It is in fact quite remarkable that a nation with so much culture should exude so little of it when they travel abroad: kebab houses, bazouki music and Demis Roussos hardly being among the greatest contributions to world civilization.

3

ARRIVALS: HOW TO ANNOY TOURISTS AT THE HARBOUR AND AIRPORT

Note

The annoyance of new arrivals into Britain became part of government policy in 1986 with the introduction of new visa requirements for many non-British passport holders. For further details and information on other ways of annoying new arrivals please contact:

CUSTOMS HOUSE
Passenger Control
Heathrow Airport
LONDON

HOW TO ANNOY NEW ARRIVALS AT THE AIRPORT

● Point at their suitcase, scream and dive for cover.

● Point at their jacket pocket, scream and dive for cover.

● Point at their trouser flies, scream and dive for cover.

● Walk up to them with arms open and hug them warmly. Overruling all their protestations drag them off to your car for a family reunion. Fifty miles down the M1, with their complaints rising, pretend at last to understand that they are not the people you thought them to be. Apologize for your actions profusely, and dump them unceremoniously on the hard shoulder with directions on how to hitch their way back to London.

● Walk up to them furtively and direct them to a plush limousine parked, engine purring, outside. Bundle them swiftly inside the vehicle then, as the vehicle speeds away from the airport with blinds drawn, tell them it is now safe for them to hand over the 'substances'. When they protest that they have no knowledge of what you are talking about reply that you are not in the mood for fun and games and make grim references to the fate of other couriers who tried to get smart.

● Walk up to them pointedly and ask them when they're thinking of leaving the country. When they reply, draw out a wad of notes and offer them money to leave earlier.

● Approach them with flowers and a film crew in close pursuit, then at the last moment as they stand pleasantly bemused to receive the gifts turn sharply away and greet someone else.

● Take hold of their suitcases while they are in the customs shed and smear the sides with the scent of a bitch you know to be on heat. Now allow them to retake possession of their luggage unaware of its new scent. Their journey home will be well and truly ruined by the constant procession of randy dogs appearing from nowhere and trying to mate with the suitcases. (Works best with Gucci.)

● Fit an RB 2-11 jet aircraft engine to the end of the moving walkway in the arrivals hall (get a friend to help you if you're not an aviation engineer) and switch the newly adapted walkway on to full thrust when the unsuspecting guest sets foot on it. Fit up a safety net some three hundred yards down the terminal to catch the airborne travellers. As an additional annoyance you could alternate between forward and reverse thrust, thus tossing the unwelcome arrivals backwards and forwards like ping pong balls.

● Casually point to the cars outside in the car park and ask in the most patronizing voice possible if the new arrivals have ever seen anything like those in their country.

● Approach a new arrival in an official manner and advise them that they are required to take certain medical tests for AIDS, rabies, black death, foot and mouth, cloven hoof, etc. Inform them that the test is very simple and that all they are required to do is provide a small urine sample. Having got their consent hand over a fifteen-gallon drum and ask them to fill it. Before they can protest direct them to the nearest broom cupboard and lock them inside, telling them to knock when they have finished. Check after three days to see how they are getting on. When they at last emerge explain there is a slight delay at the labs and they will have to remain at the airport for two weeks until the results are known. There is a risk that they may become abusive and demand to know what they can possibly do stuck in an airport for two weeks. Should this happen simply hand them another two drums and direct them back to the broom cupboard.

● Walk up to any new arrival carrying a bottle of champagne and a hotel room key and explain that they are required to take a virginity test. If they protest then point out that it is British law and explain that it shouldn't take more than six nights to carry out the tests.

HOW TO ANNOY NEW ARRIVALS AT THE HARBOUR

● After a particularly rough crossing swagger through the customs hall munching a plate of jellied eels and mussels.

● Delay docking to allow just the minimum time necessary to make any rail connection, then delay the departure of the train for a further three-quarters of an hour to irritate and annoy those breathless red-faced athletes who raced across town to make the vital connection.

● Stand at the quay waving frantically to complete strangers on board the arriving ferry.

● Go on strike (National Union Of Seamen).

● Go on strike (National Union Of Railwaymen).

● Go on strike (Customs Officers' Association).

● Employ a ventriloquist to throw his voice across the Customs shed and make the sound of a parrot squawking come out of some innocent foreigner's suitcase.

● Employ the same ventriloquist to ensure that the phrase, 'I done it, I tried to smuggle the bird into the country, it's a fair cop,' comes out of the foreigner's lips when he opens his mouth to reply to the Customs Officer's enquiry.

4

LONDON AT WAR

INTRODUCTION

Few places suffer as badly as London from the tourist onslaught. Much of the central area has been hit so badly by 'Tourist Blight' that none but a tourist would ever venture there.

To cope with this unwanted invasion Londoners require special help. To this end we now present a selective index of the principal tourist locations and the tactics to be adopted there.

THE PITFALLS AND PERILS OF TOURISTS IN LONDON

The Frontage To Buckingham Palace

It is not unknown for it to take an innocent passer-by up to half-an-hour to negotiate this 200-yard stretch of pavement. Frantic groups of Swedes and Norwegians thrust ever-heaving Hasselblads into your un-occupied passing hands. Before a protest can be lodged, the seven separate functions necessary to operate the camera have been clearly explained, in Norwegian, and you find yourself looking unhappily down the lens at a group of gum-numbing Nordic smiles arranged around the palace gates.

Confronted with this same scenario for the third time in five minutes you soon exhaust your tolerance, trading it in for one of several other responses. For a start you can carefully follow to the letter all the instructions given, all up to the last (remove the lens cap). Alternatively you can simply forget all seven instructions entirely; the result will e the same. Your reward won't, unfortunately, be immedi-ate, but rest assured that in two weeks' time your efforts will be repaid on the blank screen of some Scandinavian home projector.

The more adventurously inclined can try a more daring ploy. Walk backwards from the group, camera poised, as if you are looking for that perfect focal length. When you are some two hundred yards distant and a good way down Birdcage Walk, turn smartly, wave, pocket the camera, and make a run for it. It should be possible to evade your pursuers, leaving you the proud owner of a much-prized Hasselblad. For the truly daring one last shot of the startled visitors as they realize your deception would be well worth it for the collection.

The final and most daring ploy is to gently direct your ever-grinning guests, a few steps at a time, away from their present backcloth of the palace in a curve of some 180° so that their backs line up against the steady rush of passing traffic. A few unwitting steps backwards and a passing London bus should do the rest.

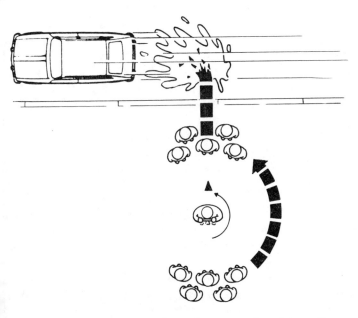

It is as well to remember that manslaughter charges could be brought against those who encourage the deaths of

foreign tourists. Do be discreet. Above all avoid taking
pictures of the ensuing carnage that could implicate you
Do not return to the scene of the incident for at least three
weeks.

The London Underground

Few situations can cause the working Londoner more irritation than a party of thirty Japanese tourists crowding
around the ticket collector's window at a busy tube station,
each attempting to pay an excess fare they don't even owe
with thirty £50 notes. Were normal commuters to engage in
such a ceremony the morning rush hour would not be
finished before three in the afternoon, and the afternoon
rush hour would barely be over before the next morning one
started.

It is simply not good enough to say that foreign tourists
should be ignored: unlike wasps and wild animals there is
simply no chance of them ever going away. Better to take
the offensive from the start. Begin with elementary propa-
ganda. Offer bogus advice to would-be travellers. At inter-
changes guide them in the opposite direction to the one they
require. At non-interchange stations make do with directing
any tourists on to the wrong platform. Better still direct
them off the platform completely. Where you have the
chance suggest a change of line at some point. And this
should be possible even with the simplest of journeys, try
and suggest an interchange where you know lift repairs are
taking place. Keep the list of these stations foremost in your
mind: a lift repair after all means long delays, or better
still, a heart-pounding walk to the surface up the safety
stairs by the unwitting foreign visitor.

Make a mental list of the stations where interchange is
difficult or impossible. Baker Street, for example, confuses
many regular travellers. Changing from the Jubilee to the
Piccadilly lines at Green Park necessitates a long and tiring
walk between platforms.

Learn too about the complexities of the Northern Line.
Send tourists to the City when they want the West End.
Dispatch them towards High Barnet when they are heading
for Hampstead and their confusion will be a joy to all non-
tourists sharing their carriage. Tell them *not* to change

trains at Elephant and Castle, and see them hurtling back through the tunnels to exactly where they started from.

Make up a black list of trouble spots and encourage the unwary towards them. Discover the joy of sending a foreigner up the wrong branch of the Piccadilly Line, bask in the sheer pleasure of directing a gullible guest to a full circuit of the Circle Line to reach a stop two stations along in the other direction.

If you can't offer misinformation at any point then satisfy yourself with basic guerrilla tactics: the briefcase if correctly balanced on the upper knee can direct a blow of considerable force into the small of any lingering tourist's back. Use this on escalators or crowded platforms to plough a furrow.

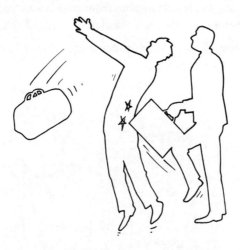

Where tourists stand on the wrong side of an escalator step smartly behind them and cough loudly down their ear. If correctly executed the effect can be quite devastating. Tourists and belongings will be sent tumbling up, or down, the escalator, or better still, both!

Never, repeat *never*, offer your seat to a foreign tourist. Linger in the warm glow of self-satisfaction when you see a foreign visitor struggle to control his bags, his camera, his pocket map of the Underground and anything else he may have to hand while you sit impassively observing his predicament. Should he stumble or fall upon you scowl blackly and stare fiercely into his eyes.

Make it a point of pride to enter any carriage before the tourist. Be aware of the value of the automatic doors: occasionally you may be rewarded by the sight of the unwary foreigner standing passively by as the train draws into and out of the station without him ever realizing there is a button to be pushed to make the doors open. More opportunist is the commuter who stands by the doors and whenever a tourist rushes to board simply presses the 'close' button drawing the doors firmly across the poor creature's face. It is a simple yet effective trick that has been perfected over the years by London Transport guards and is now available to passengers on the newer carriages.

Finally, if all else fails and you cannot maim, kill or otherwise confuse the tube-travelling visitor to our shores, then there is a basic action plan from which everyone should be able to select at least one vindictive piece of trickery:

1. Open your paper wide and across the face of any neighbour not from these shores.

2. If unwitting foreign passengers attempt to smoke, wait until the cigarette is fully alight before you point towards the no smoking sticker, thus ensuring a full cigarette is wasted as it is stubbed out.
3. If addressed in any way refuse to offer an acknowledgement.
4. When tourists have used a second seat for luggage look pointedly at the seat and ask if it is taken. Do so even when the carriage is practically empty and there are plenty of other seats.

5. When tourists are sitting beside you ensure you gain full use of the armrest (an Englishman's home is his armrest). If you are accompanied sit either side of the foreign victim and adopt the sandwich strategy:

THE SANDWICH

6. If a tourist offers you his ticket and points at the name on it seeking direction, simply nod, offer your thanks, take hold of it and walk off.

Bogus Information

One of the most profitable sources of fun for any tourist-hater is supplying bogus information to unwary tube travellers. The opportunities are great. Here are some examples.

Non-existent stations

Try suggesting that a journey starts or finishes at one of the following non-existent underground stations:

● BELGRAVE PARK
● HAMPTON CIRCUS

- THE THAMES
- MARY POPPINS
- HARRODS LONDON
- MARKS AND SPENCER
- BIRMINGHAM

Outstanding stations

Recommend one of the following stations as particularly worth a visit for its architectural charm and merit:

- BRIXTON
- DAGENHAM EAST
- NEW CROSS
- NEASDEN
- HOUNSLOW CENTRAL

Bogus lines

Considerable confusion may be caused by advising a journey on a line that simply doesn't exist. Among those to suggest are:

- THE CORONATION LINE
- THE CENTRAL DISTRICT LINE
- THE CITY AND TOWN LINE

Restricted service

It is good policy to point out that certain stations operate a restricted service and are only open on prior application. Explain to would-be travellers they should phone the station master to arrange an appointment beforehand when planning to use the following stations:

- OXFORD CIRCUS
- BANK
- WATERLOO
- KING'S CROSS ST PANCRAS

Special information

The following special information should be passed on to travellers using the tube service for the first time:

Request Stop: Many trains only stop at a station if the travellers on the platform request it to stop. To stop a train entering the station walk to the edge of the platform and put your hand out to signal to the oncoming driver that you wish to board the train.

Open Top Trains: During the summer months London Transport operates a number of open-top tubes for special sightseeing runs. Please contact the nearest Underground station for details.

To Book a Tube: Where a group of people are travelling together they may book a private tube for any journey lasting longer than five stops. Contact London Transport Passenger Services for further information.

Guards: It is normal to tip the guard an average of 10% of the total fare upon completion of the journey. The guard is to be found in the rear carriage of any train.

OPEN TOP BUSES

1. Few people boarding open-top buses ever travel on the lower deck. This should give ample opportunities for the tourist-hater to get to work. Start by assembling a sturdy party of men, the heavier the better. Board the bus and make for the lower deck which you should find empty. Wait for the bus to start, then move to one side of the vehicle causing it to tilt in that direction.

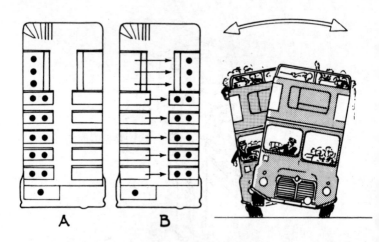

Wait a few seconds for the new centre of gravity to be established, then move smartly and efficiently to the opposite side of the vehicle causing it to tilt sharply the other way. Repeat the procedure until the journey ceases or until all passengers from the upper deck have left in a state of nervous distress.

Do warn the driver and conductor of your proposals. It is unfair that they should suffer unwittingly. Indeed you may find they want to join in.

2. The wash-wipe trick. The wash-wipe fitted to the bus and normally directed at the wind-screen can be modified to direct the jet of water away from the screen and directly upwards into the air. The result when the bus is in motion is a fine spray of drizzle over the upper deck which makes passengers rush for shelter.

The trick has an added advantage, for with the screen wash inoperative the driver is likely to quickly suffer loss of vision. The increased likelihood of an accident occurring can only be of benefit if it spoils the fun of any tourist passengers on board. The heroic self-sacrifice of the London Transport drivers is a shining example to us all.

Further Bus Advice

Upon entering

Should you spot a foreigner entering a bus that is quite full, then it is always a good idea to suggest that there might be more room below stairs in 'the cellar'. Direct him towards the luggage space beneath the stairs, pointing out that this is the way to the cellar stairs. Before he realizes his error ring smartly on the bell causing the bus to pull away with the hapless foreigner trapped with the luggage. With any luck it will be several minutes before he is able to secure his release. Try and organize a competition with friends to see who can direct the greatest number of foreigners into the 'cellar' in one go. The record stands at a party of twenty-six Japanese holidaymakers who remained trapped for three hours.

The bell

Explain that the bell is used for calling in-flight assistance and that a sharp ring on the bell will summon the conductor/conductress for light refreshments, meals, drinks and hostess service, in much the same way that the air stewardess is called in an aeroplane. Explain that being half-throttled by a burly bus driver after you have ordered two Scotch and drys and a round of club sandwiches is just a traditional English pastime to which no heed should be paid.

Stopping a bus

Take the first opportunity to indicate to foreign guests the correct manner for stopping a bus, namely that you should stand out from the kerb waving two fingers vigorously at the driver's cab in a firm and positive manner. Assure guests that not only will the bus always stop for a signal given like this, but that the driver will actually leave his cab to address you personally.

Safety drill

Should you be lucky enough to be on board a bus heading towards Tower Bridge, then leap to your feet as the bridge comes into sight and give a complete life-saving drill as though you were on board an aircraft. Explain how to inflate the life-jackets under the seats and explain the correct procedure for disembarking if forced to ditch at sea. Finish by holding a prayer meeting. Watch for the mad scramble to the safety exits.

Bus numbers

Few tourists ever come to grips with bus numbers. The simple reason is that in most towns all buses look remarkably similar and to distinguish one from another is often impossible. To this end a simple ploy can be suggested. Guide the tourist to the bus stop and direct him to the correct bus. Ensure that he boards the bus required then leave him with the advice that upon leaving the bus at the other end he should attempt to mark it in some prominent manner in order that he might be able to recognize it again later and thus make the return journey home. Suggest that he uses some mark that is easily visible. There can be few things that inflame a bus driver more than leaving his bus at the terminus for a well-deserved rest only to discover some foreign tourist scrawling his name down the side of the vehicle with a bold felt-tip pen.

VICTORIA COACH STATION

The coach station is such a maze of confusion that it is unlikely you will have to do anything constructive to cause any further mayhem. No one ever appears to know where anything is or which coaches are going where. Indeed most drivers often seem doubtful about where they are going and have to pop out to check the destination board at the front of their coach before they leave to see for themselves. Under these circumstances you can proffer any advice you care in the certain knowledge it will only add to the recipient's distress.

Remember that each year the manager at Victoria Coach station offers a V.C. medal (a Victoria Coach station medal) to that person causing the greatest inconvenience to a foreign traveller over the preceding twelve months. At present the title goes to a gentleman who managed to dispatch an unwary traveller to Aberdeen and back despite the fact that he had only popped into the station to pick up something from left luggage. Direct all competitors to the manager.

Remember that Victoria Coach station is just that sufficient distance from the railway station to make any transfer, especially with luggage, an awkward and tiring affair. What's more the local geography makes it easy to capitalize on this. What may normally be an awkward quarter-mile jaunt can, when misdirected to the full, take up to several miles and be totally fatiguing. Those conversant with the area will no doubt wish to offer their own suggestions. For those less well equipped the unwary traveller should be directed along the route illustrated here.

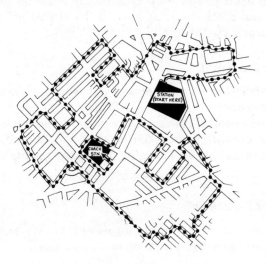

N.B: The advice here is for a trip from rail to coach station. For the reverse journey simply offer the instructions in reverse order. Or for added effect re-arrange the instructions in any order you fancy for maximum confusion.

PEN PIX OF LONDON

The following sights are highly recommended for referring foreign guests and visitors to.

The Tower

Often called The Bloody Tower, because those visiting are apt to emerge after seeing it and exclaim, 'Well, I didn't bloody well think much of that.'

The British Museum

Megalithic old fossil of unrivalled tedium. And that's just the outside; wait till you go inside!

Kew Gardens

Botanic gardens of rare beauty, disturbed somewhat by the constant presence of low-flying aircraft on their final approach to Heathrow Airport some five miles up the road. Be sure and check flight paths with the airport beforehand to ensure any visit is totally ruined.

St Paul's Cathedral

Domed structure of some appeal but whose environs lack charm or feature. A visit to the Whispering Gallery, up an interminable spiral staircase, is especially recommended to those visitors with heart conditions and weight problems, or those carrying heavy shopping and wearing high-heeled shoes.

Houses of Parliament

Anywhere that is best known for its appearance on a sauce bottle label cannot surely be up to all that much.

Cleopatra's Needle

Phallic lump of rock totally lacking in interest or appeal. In another era it would surely rank as no more than a bridge support on some motorway intersection.

Greenwich Observatory

A superficially entertaining but ultimately rather disappointing landmark reached only by a tortuous cross-town journey. The lasting problem with all observatories is that astronomy is unfortunately an extremely dull and boring subject and despite its lavish setting, Greenwich, like the rest, must fail to excite.

Marble Arch

Once a notable landmark, now converted to a road traffic island.

The London Planetarium

Basically the same as Greenwich but without the benefit of the setting. The Planetarium has made noble attempts to bring the world of astronomy into the Eighties. Unfortunately despite all their efforts it still remains resolutely dull.

Trafalgar Square

Despite a number of impressive buildings around its sides Trafalgar Square is unfortunately no more than a glorified patio, albeit with pigeons and a two-hundred-foot monument. But just like any patio it has little noticeable appeal. It can best be enjoyed by tourists when crowded with police and demonstrators, especially during a baton charge. Or during a frantic crowd surge on New Year's Eve with drunks and pickpockets grabbing at every garment.

The Statue of Eros

Fashioned after the Greek God of love, Eros is now a favourite haunt of drug pushers and male prostitutes.

Soho

Formerly the lurid porn centre of the capital, now greatly cleaned up. Hence the reason for its complete lack of interest.

Carnaby Street

The once-fashionable swinging Sixties street has perfectly retained its appearance and character. Hence the reason it is so unpopular nowadays.

Tower Bridge

Famous bridge, now with own museum that commands excellent views but very little else.

Albert Hall

Victorian seating and Victorian acoustics combine to make an arena that only a Victorian pugilist would appreciate.

Oxford Street

A two-mile taxi rank with wall-to-wall shoe shops.

Portobello Market

While over in Britain it is a good idea to suggest that guests catch part of 'real' London. A part the locals go to. Doubtless your suggestion will be taken up and a visit to Portobello Market arranged. They may have difficulty finding it: a member of BATA who sells flowers in Notting Hill Gate has the right idea – 'Don't ask me where Portobello Road is, buy a map.' It is only if they finally arrive at the market that they realize that 'real' London comprises 'real' pickpocketing, 'real' mugging, 'real' street crime, and 'real' drug pushers.

Madame Tussaud's

There was a time when people visited Madame Tussaud's and came away uncomplaining. This was before the television era, when none of us knew what famous people actually looked like. With the advent of the mass media we are less willing to take a collection of wax dummies to be quite the true likenesses they purport to be.

Covent Garden

Once a thriving fruit market, now Covent Garden is given over to the nouvelle yuppy and haute touriste. It is designed exclusively for the tourist with every possible care taken to cater for their needs. It is consequently the last place any tourist should visit.

5

THE BATTLE FOR BRITAIN

Part of the BATA advertising campaign for European cities

THE BATTLE FOR BRITAIN

London may be in the front line of attack in any tourist onslaught but other cities are equally besieged – York, Cambridge, Oxford, Edinburgh, Bath, Canterbury and Stratford. It is to these battle-weary stations that we now turn our attention.

York

Tourist York comprises two principal features: the Shambles, and the assorted historical remains littered around the city. For the most part the latter offer the greatest potential for the tourist-hater. Ancient remains remain stubbornly unenlightening. Let's face it, when you've seen one Roman ruin being excavated then you've seen them all. One archaeological dig tends to look much like any other dig after a while. Try directing tourists toward any gas or sewage repairs. Explain that this is a genuine site of historical interest. See how long it takes before they lose interest and wander off.

Misdirection is a useful ploy in York. The Shambles, as the name implies is a shambles to negotiate. Don't bother to misdirect here; it will happen naturally. But there is fun to be had. Try giving out directions that actually bring the lost visitor back to where he started from. Stay on the spot and wait for him or her to return. Make a point of stressing that your instructions cannot have been properly followed – this will ensure that the footweary traveller feels not only lost but guilty. Repeat your instructions, this time directing your victim on an altogether different route. Again wait for your plans to work their circuitous course. As the dejected alien appears for the second time, throw up your arms in horror, claiming that you have never met anyone with such a poor sense of geography. Refuse to re-direct for a third time, passing your charge to a fellow local who can take over where you left off and also enjoy these 'boomerang' ploys.

York has a useful Minster much fancied by tourists. There is little you can do to interfere with those visiting a place of God like this, but try standing by the honesty box at the entrance scowling heavily at any who walk past without paying. You'd be amazed how many will feel compelled to cough up. The Minster undercroft houses the wonderful cathedral treasures, and just like all wonderful cathedral treasures they are singularly dull.

York has two famous citizens – Guy Fawkes and Dick Turpin – which should give you a pretty shrewd idea of what the local people are like. The Castle Street Museum recreates a bygone way of life though many foreign tourists, notably the French, probably still live in places like that. The Railway Museum is now a major feature in the city, attracting steam enthusiasts from all over the country. So if that's not a good enough reason to give it a miss, Lord knows what is.

Bath

Like York, Bath has a selection of ancient artefacts. Once again, without exception, they fail to live up to expectations. Mind you, it is difficult to know what exactly we do expect. If we were wise we would realize that the Roman bath-house – a sort of two-thousand-year-old swimming baths – would be unlikely to captivate for long. After all, who would want to visit any of our present municipal swimming baths in two thousand years' time? Having failed to find our imagination satisfied by a few feet of stagnant, murky, green water, we now go in search of the Nash terraces, only to discover that one Nash terrace starts to look very like another Nash terrace, after a short while – just as a room crammed full of Old Masters tends to dilute their impact to the point where we scarcely cast an eye at them. Add to this a chronic shortage of parking places which requires the motorist to start queuing on Thursday for a parking spot on Saturday week, and you can feel the appeal of Bath slowly slipping away.

Of course Bath is a beautiful city – there is no denying it. Nor is there any chance of denying the determined foreign sightseers who flock there for a chance of appreciating that beauty. What we must do then is deflect the tourists' attention towards some other, possibly non-existent, target. Thus we encourage visitors to take in the *real* Bath, the Bath that few tourists see. Explain that by travelling a little way east they will be able to see a part of Bath that everyone else misses. No matter that everyone else misses it because it isn't there. Persuade them not to stay with the traditional sights – the Pump House, the Royal Crescent, the Assembly Rooms, beautiful though they are – but to hire a cab and see the parts that are really memorable. Send them packing off in the direction of the ancient Roman city of Swindon. By the time they realize there is nothing to see they will be so dispirited that they will have little interest in the whole affair and will leave without ever bothering about the majesty they missed.

For those who care to note, four miles out of Bath is the American museum at Claverton. Period rooms and furnishings give a picture of American life in the seventeenth to nineteenth centuries, including an exhibition of authentic Red Indian art which is of great interest to anyone who wants to know what a genuine Red Indian tepee set in the grounds of a Georgian English manor house might look like.

Canterbury

The advantage of Canterbury for the tourist-hater is that the bulk of the work is already done for you. Here is a town with little to offer but which features on most tour itineraries. Apart from the cathedral and its precincts, there is frankly bugger all to see here – aside from a one-way system that reduces the town to a six-lane race track, and a series of gaudy gift shops featuring every conceivable use of the name 'Chaucer' plus several inconceivable ones to boot. Incidentally, Canterbury Cathedral is famous as the cathedral where Thomas à Becket was laid to rest. Not that there's actually anything left to see – King Henry made sure of that by getting rid of the tomb (obviously he'd had a bad day in Canterbury too) – but there is a bit of worn pavement where the tomb used to be. So if you like looking at worn paving slabs, then this is definitely the place for you.

The town still has the remains of its ancient city walls, which give a commanding view over . . . er, the ring road, and there is a Norman keep, a Saxon church and a Roman mosaic pavement, just in case you're looking for something to fill another five minutes. The trick then is to suggest a full-day excursion here. Sell the virtues of the town. Beg, plead, insist that the visitor allow no less than a full day for his trip. Thus primed, the tripper will reach Canterbury bright and early to find it somewhat less than brimming with the interest he or she had bargained for. After a quick look round they will start with the cathedral, planning to take the rest of the town in later, only to find that by ten o'clock they have covered the whole town twice, been three times round the crypt, and spent three quarters of an hour in the Geoffrey Chaucer tea rooms trying to think what to do with the rest of the day.

Cambridge

High on the tourist agenda Cambridge is a source of rich pickings for the tourist-hater. Start with a simple yet effective trick.For instance, it is a good idea to make a list of the best colleges to recommend visitors to see.

Girton
Several miles from the city centre, Girton is of nondescript character. Advise any visitor that it is no more than a five-minute walk from the railway station.

Churchill
A starkly new college with little of the appeal of the more traditional ones, Churchill is sufficient distance from the centre to make any detour an irritation.

Fitzwilliam
A characterless college again of sufficient distance out of town to be annoying.

Fitzjohns

A nonexistent college well worth enlarging upon. A fruitless search is certain to cause hours of spoilt happiness.

Recommendation of any of these colleges is certain to have an unhappy effect on those taking your advice.

Punting

Few tourists will be able to resist the chance of a go at punting. In many ways it is pointless to interfere. They will make such an awful mess anyway that they are best left to their own devices. Where advice is felt necessary try the following. Stand as far to the rear of the boat as possible and drop the pole firmly into the water pressing it down into the river bed as far as it will go to gain a decent leverage. Push against the static pole to propel the boat forward through the water at the same time pulling the pole from its hole. Repeat. The illustration shows the likely result of such a routine.

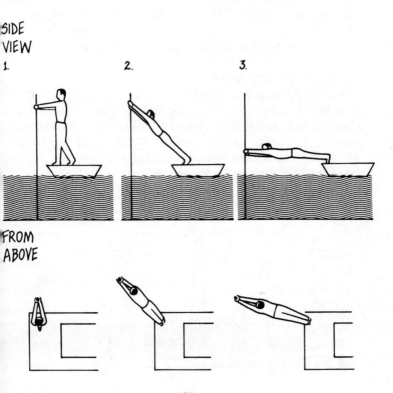

SIDE VIEW

1.   2.   3.

FROM ABOVE

Bike Hire

Bicycle hire is popular amongst tourists in Cambridge. Should you suspect a passing bicyclist is of tourist origin you should walk or drive smartly out into their path. The rider will immediately take evasive action resulting in no little discomforture. On no account commit such an act in front of resident bikes. Resident cyclists will take no avoiding action and will simply continue riding in your general direction, a most alarming prospect.

Oxford

Much of what has been said about Cambridge may be equally well employed in Oxford. Bogus or far-flung colleges are again worth a recommendation. Or suggest a delightful walk in the pretty, cloistered suburb of Cowley. Like Cambridge, Oxford has a river and opportunities to punt. Remember the Oxford style is to punt from the middle of the boat – a less satisfactory arrangement for the tourist-hater since it allows little opportunity for catastrophe. It may therefore be necessary to resort to more mischievous means to disrupt the erstwhile punter's progress.

The Rubber Punting Pole

It consists of an ordinary punting pole sawn in half, with a stout rubber tube inserted in the middle. The pole feels like a normal pole and indeed, behaves like one too, until strong pressure is applied to one end, at which point the whole thing acts like a whiplash catapulting the unwary punter out of the boat and across the water.

1. 2. 3.

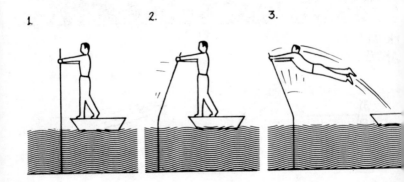

Clearly caution has to be used in substituting the one pole for the other. This caution is amply repaid though by the results that accrue.

Edinburgh

Scotland's historic capital is renowned for its annual festival of music and drama. For the rest of the year it is renowned for being a major drug-traffic centre. The best possible advice to give any foreign tourist thinking of taking in the city is to visit during the Festival month. Explain that accommodation is bountiful at this time and that there is no need to book ahead. Explain the generosity of the Scots. Do not explain that the nearest 'room vacant' sign they will find is liable to be in Carlisle and that even this is likely to be a shared laundry cupboard with a seven-man alternative comedy mime group from the University of East Anglia who insist on practising their act in the hotel lounge. Besides the festival, Edinburgh has a magnificent castle that stands proudly at the top of the Royal Mile and boasts a large museum. If you like thirty-seven rooms full of military medals and an entire wing devoted to ancient armoury, then this is the place for you. If you don't then spare yourself the coronary and persuade a foreigner to go in your place. Below the castle in Princes Street stands the Scott monument, while nearby is the Royal National Gallery of Scotland, the Royal Scottish Academy, the Royal Scottish Museum, and the National Library of Scotland. It is one of the pervading mysteries of life that whilst the Scots and the Welsh can dwell and linger on national pride in this way, if the English were to do likewise it would be seen as unsavoury and jingoistic to the extreme. Nonetheless the effect of such an overburdening weight of Hibernian fervour soon saturates even the most willing tourist, who quickly runs screaming from the city in search of a non-tartan haven.

Stratford

Home of Shakespeare, shrine to the immortal bard, sanctuary of the lover of fine words and prose, and a pretty awful traffic bottleneck thanks to Sir Hugh Clopton's medieval stone bridge. Much of Stratford is half-timbered save for the theatre itself, which was built in 1932 and looks like an air raid shelter. Shakespeare's birthplace is preserved as too is Halls Croft, where the poet's daughter lived; Anne Hathaway's cottage, where Anne Hathaway lived; Mary Arden's house, where Mary Arden lived; and Holy Trinity church, where Shakespeare now lies. Indeed, perhaps the only thing to do with Shakespeare that isn't preserved is Shakespeare himself. With such a plethora of Shakespearean remains around, it is not difficult for the would-be tourist-baiter to set to work describing where Shakespeare first snogged with a girl, where Shakespeare first went skinny-dipping in the River Avon, where Shakespeare first did a moonie out of a car window. Well, you take the point; with a little imagination there is little Shakespeare didn't do if you put your tongue to it.

In reality most people come to Stratford for the theatre, and the best and most foolproof way of ruining their visit is close at hand. We print below the endings to all Shakespeare's major works. Check which work is playing at the theatre that night and make it your objective to give away that ending to as many people as possible. In shops, in pubs, walking down the street, talk loudly and clearly. Make sure you are overheard by anyone within a fifty-foot range. You will be amazed at how such a small thing can completely ruin an evening at the theatre.

Shakespeare – The Endings

The Merchant Of Venice   Portia and Nerissa save the day. Antonio's ships arrive safe and well and Shylock becomes a Christian.

King Lear   Regan is poisoned, Goneril commits suicide, Cordelia is hanged, Lear dies from grief and Albany takes over the kingdom.

The Taming Of The Shrew   The shrew is tamed. The end.

Romeo and Juliet   Mercutio is killed, Romeo takes poison, Juliet stabs herself.

Richard III   Richard is killed in battle. Richmond becomes king.

A Midsummer Night's Dream   Helena marries Demetrius. Hermia marries Lysander. Everyone lives happily ever after.

Hamlet   The following die: Hamlet, Gertrude, Claudius, Laertes, Ophelia and Polonius, Rosencrantz and Guildenstern.

The Tempest   Prospero frees Ariel from service, renounces magic, and leaves Caliban alone on the island.

Antony and Cleopatra   Antony falls on his sword. Cleopatra takes her own life with the aid of an asp. The asp lives happily ever after.

Macbeth   Lady Macduff is slaughtered, Macduff kills Macbeth.

The Two Gentlemen Of Verona   Valentine marries Silvia, Proteus returns, everyone lives happily ever after.

The Comedy Of Errors   Egeon recovers his two sons and his liberty and the abbess turns out to be his lost wife Emilia.

Julius Caesar   Brutus and Cassius top themselves.

Twelfth Night   Olivia marries Cesario. The Duke marries Viola.

Measure For Measure   Everyone gets married to everyone else in the end.

All's Well That Ends Well   Helena explains all about the ring and marries Bertram.

Take these notes with you when visiting Stratford for additional support. Read clearly and slowly and in a prominent public position where you will effect maximum damage.

NB: Those finding it difficult to get the plot endings correct should not worry. If in doubt simply invent any plausible ending. The damage will still be done for those unlucky enough to overhear will be so confused when the plot you have implanted in their mind fails to match the one on the stage in front of them that they are quite likely never to visit the town again.

6

AT THE SEASIDE

AT THE SEASIDE

Annoying foreigners at the seaside isn't always that easy. For a start at a quick glance all seaside visitors can appear strangely similar. It is wise, therefore to prepare oneself thoroughly beforehand and to acquaint oneself with the differences. Foreign guests to our seashores can normally be identified by reference to the following features.

Tan

Most foreign visitors have a far better tan than their British counterparts. Indeed their British counterparts would probably not have tans at all were it not for previous foreign holidays. Puffy red raw skin is a peculiar British trademark brought about by the very small number of sunny days during the British summer. The briefest appearance of the sun on a summer's day can result in the most frantic scramble of sunbathers anxious to take advantage before the chance is lost. This is quite unlike the example of our continental neighbours who can afford to tan more slowly, secure in the knowledge that there will be regular sunshine. The British sun-seeker must grab every opportunity available even if this leads to chronic sunstroke and a body the colour of a lightly boiled lobster. Look out especially for swollen pink flesh and the slapping sound of the constant application of suntan cream. Now look out for those not falling into this category. These are your foreign guests.

Beachwear

It is a sad fact of life that the British lag well behind the rest of the world in their dress sense on the beach. Indeed with the exception of the odd Eastern European country, and the occasional third world state, it is fair to say Britain comes securely at the bottom of the dress sense league. Typical items to look out for on the British body are overlarge bathing trunks, possibly with the edge of a pair of underpants exposed beneath, towelling changing robes made from old curtains (with or without the curtain rail still attached), rubber bathing caps with flower detail attached (often with a number of the flowers missing), open 'Jesus style' sandals worn with socks beneath, beenie hats often with unsavoury messages prominently displayed, pot-bellied T-shirts likewise decorated, cardigans, jumpers and other woollen garments worn despite the presence of a blazing sun, brief swimming garments worn despite the lack of a blazing sun, rolled up trouser legs, knotted hand-kerchieves, nose shields, vests and braces.

British dress sense is occasionally matched by that of American visitors, but even they somehow manage to carry off their brash outfits with more aplomb.

Should you spot a sunseeker with any or indeed all of the items referred to above then it is safe to assume they are of native origin. Cast your eyes elsewhere in search of tourist targets.

Food

An excellent barometer of nationality. Look for the crudely-formed sandwiches, the jumbo plastic bottle of pop (often partially deformed from the sun, and often with a thin sediment of sand in the bottom) and melted ice creams with a sprinkling of sand on the top, and you've hit upon the British family. It is a peculiarity of the British that they feel compelled to eat almost continually. Especially when on holiday. A crude method of identification is to take your watch and time the interval between snacks. If the family in question go for longer than twenty minutes without food passing their lips then the chances are they are foreign.

Shape

Again it is a sad fact of life that the British family are always those with the least physically attractive appearnce. They are not necessarily the fattest, that honour must go to the Germans and Americans. Nor are they necessarily the most wimpish. It is just that when assembled together en masse the British reveal a national trait that is altogether unappealing. It is as though the British body has not been built for the outdoors and that exposure to it brings out this inadequacy to the full. Watch the way they stumble across the sand laden down with half a ton of beach furniture and enough reading matter to last a lifetime. Anyone not conforming to this norm is likely to be foreign.

Other Features

The tan line
The tell-tale tan is peculiarly unique to the British. It marks the first removal of a particular garment that year and marks the divide between exposed and unexposed flesh. Look for it around the base of the neck and the upper arms. Presence of a prominent tan line denotes home nationality.

Beachcraft
Only the British feel compelled to build castles and sand workings on the beach. The reason is unclear. Some might argue it is a national preoccupation with defence, others that it is simply a product of the British climate that makes any form of vigorous exercise a necessity. Either way it is a safe bet that the family at present excavating the better part of the beach area is British and those looking on in bemused silence are foreign.

Bathing
Sea bathing in Britain is not something undertaken for enjoyment's sake. It is something which one embarks upon as a challenge, a way of purging body and soul alike. It is done so one can proudly boast that one achieved it. This immediately marks out the British bather from his foreign partner for the foreigner bathes because he enjoys it, and there is no way he could possibly enjoy the sub-zero waters that lap around our shores. He will restrict himself to the occasional paddle, if that, and will look on with a genuinely pained expression as others take to the waters. It is a safe bet therefore that anyone spotted in the water is British.

Nude Sunbathing

Alas the British have still not adapted to the art of nude bathing and feel ill at ease in such circumstances. They are likely to go to enormous lengths to protect their privacy or else exhibit complete and wanton abandonment, exposing themselves to anyone within a full fifty miles as though they were doing no more than take off their jumper. Continental naturists, on the other hand, tend to carry these things off with a great deal more flair, treating the whole affair as though it were the most natural thing in the world. It is unlikely, given the climate of most British summers, that you will get a chance to spot this difference but it is nonetheless worth remembering.

Ten Least Pleasant Places On The Beach

Where possible foreign visitors should be encouraged or directed to pitch camp:

1. By the local sewage outfall pipe.
2. Underneath a line of unstable cliff formations.
3. Downwind from the beach toilets.
4. Six inches from a pile of rotting seaweed.
5. In a treacherous hidden cove that is quickly cut off by the sea.
6. On a stretch of beach with dangerous unmarked tidal currents.
7. Next to a family from Birmingham.
8. Three miles from the actual shoreline.
9. On the same beach as the Radio One Roadshow.
10. On any beach within 500 miles of Sellafield Nuclear Reprocessing Plant.

The Summer Outfit Trick

This is a good trick for use in boarding houses and small hotels in which a foreign family may be guests. Start by making the acquaintance of the other British families in the hotel. Let them know your position. Tell them that you have a deep and passionate hatred of foreign tourists and would do anything in your power to ruin their holiday. You are sure to find your fellow guests sympathetic. Once you have taken your fellow Englishmen into your confidence your planning can go ahead. Start by keeping a regular watch on the weather forecast. Keep an eye out for any day that promises to be particularly unpleasant or cold. When one is found quickly alert your fellow guests. Warn them to come down to breakfast next morning in the lightest possible clothes. Thin summer dresses for the women, shorts for the men. The foreign guests, on seeing everyone dressed in this way, will immediately assume that the weather is about to break and will quickly return to their rooms to change accordingly. Once you yourself are clear of the hotel you can quickly change into more appropriate clothing leaving your hapless foreign partners to struggle for warmth.

As an alternative to this you may select a day that promises to be particularly hot or humid. Dress in thick winter woollies making sure your conspiratorial partners do likewise. The hapless foreign guests will again rush to their rooms to put on heavy winter garb while you again beat a hasty retreat and slip into something more appropriate.

How to Depress

You would be surprised how easy it is to depress the spirits of foreign guests at the hotel in which you are staying. We list a few simple examples below. As a courtesy to native guests staying in the hotel we suggest you warn them of your intentions in order that they themselves may not be upset by your actions.

● Come down at breakfast wearing a black tie and arm band and sobbing loudly into a handkerchief.

● Sit in the hotel lobby alone after dinner reading loudly from a book entitled *How To Cope With Divorce*.

● Rush out to the toilet with a serviette held to the mouth just after the first course of evening dinner.

● Assume a maudlin position in the hotel bar and talk about the futility of human existence, and the probability of contracting AIDS.

- Read aloud from the obituary columns in *The Times*.

- Discuss your recent prostate operation over dinner usin
the vegetables on your plate to illustrate exactly wha
happened.

- Offer to quote passages from a book of First World Wa
poems.

- Sit in a corner reading the Bible in the hotel disco.

- Sit in the hotel lounge all day watching the school
programmes on the television.

Least Interesting Holiday Resorts

The greatest effort should be made to attract foreign tourist
to Britain's least interesting seaside resorts. They are:

Frinton-on-Sea
So dull, it carries a government health warning. The tow
has caused widespread hilarity by releasing a holida
brochure.

Grange-Over-Sands
The heart of Costa Geriatrica. Avoid on pension day, double
stamp day, and any time between January and Decembe
(inclusive). The main sights of interest in Grange are

Skegness
Lincolnshire by the sea. Was previously twinned with th
industrial Ruhr Valley town of Dusseldorf, but Dusseldor
broke off the twinning when it recognized the associatio
with Skegness wasn't doing its own image much good. Bes
places to visit when holidaying in Skegness are: Londo
Edinburgh, Spain.

Cromer
A north Norfolk coastal resort. Closed Tuesdays and Thurs
days and throughout August (key left under mat).

Morecambe
Northern seaside resort. Last year over 58,000 people vis
ited Morecambe on holiday (only 3,800 stayed longer tha

half an hour). Jokes about Morecambe's legendary dullness abound, suffice it to say none are in fact accurate. People in Morecambe do not queue up to watch the traffic lights change. After all, there's no point since it's usually an all-ticket affair.

Sidmouth
The Morecambe Of The South.
No persons admitted under sixty-five.
Half day closing – Monday to Friday.

Borth
Mid Wales. Thirty-seven miles of caravan sites and a chip shop. The native tongue in Borth is West Midlands. Borth is famous for regularly recording a wind chill factor several degrees below that which is technically possible. The best way to see the town is probably through the gunsights of a Phantom jet fighter.

Rhyl
See Rhyl and die. Better still, die first, then see Rhyl.

INTIMIDATION OF FOREIGN TOURISTS

General intimidation is the most common form of activity when wishing to annoy the seaside tourist. Loud or ill-mannered conduct, rude, noisy and abrasive behaviour are the most common approaches. Unfortunately they are often adopted by the very people you hope to annoy and may well founder for this very reason. A further course of action may therefore be necessary.

Fortunately this is readily offered by the 'Family Attack' – that is an attack by a bogus family group. This will arouse less suspicion than a BATA freedom-fighter working alone – families are after all the most common type of holiday grouping, and will therefore offer you the chance to carry off your annoyance with the greatest security. Try one of the following.

The Miserable Family Approach

You will need two adults and at least one teenage offspring, preferably in his or her late teens. You should then take to the beach, promenade, or café as a group being sure to maintain uniformly miserable faces. Remember there are few things in life more miserable than the teenage son or daughter on holiday with their parents and the sight of such a group is greeted with a look of utter dejection by most onlookers. The youngster naturally looks glum and depressed at being seen on holiday with two people who look old enough to be his or her . . . well, his or her parents to be exact. Likewise the parents for their part look equally glum at having to spend two weeks in the company of such a sullen party. The sight of the Miserable Family out together is guaranteed to upset any onlooker and immediately spoil their holiday. The thought of such pent-up misery is, after all, highly contagious to all who observe it. The miserable family can gain great satisfaction from touring the summer holiday resorts maximizing their impact and minimizing the fun of those who spot them. Even worse is the 35-year-old offspring on holiday with parents. The sight of this can induce quite morbid feelings that leave all around depressed and fed up.

The Happy Family

The exact opposite of the miserable family and yet, remarkably, the happy family are quite likely to provoke a near identical response in those exposed to them. There are few things in life more irksome than a happy, glowing, jolly family with 'matey' dad, 'bouncy' mum, and irrepressibly yukky kids. This typical 'Kelloggs' family group attempt to transplant their own brand of chummy happiness into the hearts and minds of others. It is a transplant that is doomed to failure for such family bonhomie cannot fail to provoke anything but scorn in those exposed to it. To provoke such scorn, and the feeling of general irritation it engenders you should assemble around yourself just such a family and march proudly on to the beach. You can be sure that the instant waves of nausea that hit the other bathers will sweep down the beach and leave these hapless victims feeling vaguely unwell for the rest of the day.

The Poor Family

The depression factor once again accounts for the damaging response we experience upon seeing the Poor Family on the beach. A noticeably second-hand wind-break constructed of girder iron and serge linen, and threadbare beach towels cut from old curtains bring onlookers out in a wave of melancholia. Again the trick is to assemble together a bogus family and equip them with 'poor' accessories accordingly. You could even consider buying your equipment off a genuinely poor family, thereby freeing them from their own pecuniary disadvantage while at the same time arming yourself for your own task. You don't need to take to the beach for more than a few minutes, it being quite possible to effect all the damage you wish in the shortest of interludes. The effect of the poor family is to overwhelm all onlookers with a feeling of unnecessary guilt that prevents them fully enjoying the remainder of their holiday.

The Fat Family

The effect is again immediate. As soon as the Fat Family troop on to the beach there is a communal drawing of breath. It is difficult to decide quite why. Do we despise them their fatness? Do we sympathize with their plight? Do we simply see in them all that is in ourselves and find it a little too close for comfort? Frankly it doesn't really matter. Once the fat family hit the sand we cannot enjoy quite the same peace of mind that we did before. The trick is clearly simple – assemble a crowd of fatties around you and loiter tubbishly, dripping your full quota of flab in fullest view. After the initial wave of laughter has passed, the beach will be left feeling slightly awkward, a combination perhaps of the emotional responses already described tinged with just a tiny feeling of guilt at that initial uncharitable laughter.

The Sporting Family

This is the family who cannot rest for five seconds without being compelled to jump or hit or catch or throw something. From the first second that they arrive on the beach with the equivalent of a portable multi-gym, they are the embodiment of perpetual motion. If they are not playing cricket they are playing football, and when the football finishes it is bowls, or frisbee, or beach tennis, or an elaborate version of volleyball that seems to take up virtually the entire beach. And it is not just the fact that the ball is constantly landing on some sunburnt back or that any object within a half-mile radius becomes slowly covered in a coat of sand courtesy of the unending procession of sporting feet. Nor is it the noise of the constant arguments that turn into constant sulks. Nor is it the perpetual huff and puff of sporting activity. No, the fact is the Sporting Family seem incapable of realizing that their energies can exhaust other people as well as themselves and thereby wreak ruination beyond their immediate family circle. It is difficult to assemble a bogus version of this family since to do so requires that all those taking part must virtually kill themselves in pursuit of other people's unhappiness. It is nonetheless a trump card that can occasionally be played and might succeed where other family groups fail.

The Diggers

This is the family that marches on to the beach and proceeds at once to engage in a series of elaborate earth- or rather sand-works, painstakingly constructed over a period of hours only to be washed away by the tide in as many seconds. There is a singular lack of point to the whole exercise and it is this futility, a grown man making sand castles, that causes it to upset any unfortunate onlooker. The feeling is that this man should surely be doing something more rewarding with his time other than roping his children and family into a form of rewardless slave labour. Again the problem is that you must perform several hours of back-breaking work to achieve the end in question. Indeed it is even worth considering whether the end product may be that you feel far worse than those you wish to upset. Still, for those with determination to cause psychological damage to others this trick may have its virtues.

SEASIDE TACTICS OF SPECIAL INTEREST

Sunburn

Try approaching a sunbathing couple undetected, then carefully pour the entire contents of their suntan lotion bottle on to the sand and replace with Spry Crisp'n'Dry. There is generally little difference in texture or colour. The effect over a period of hours is to gently fry the entire skin of the unsuspecting victim.

Rock

Most seaside rock has a message printed in its core. The story is now well known of a confectionery company in dispute with its workforce who took the celebrated step of changing the words inside the rock to a sexually graphic phrase inviting an act of departure. Five thousand sticks of this rock were produced with the ensuing damage to the firm's reputation. There is no need for you to wait for an industrial dispute to get hold of such rock. We feel a discreet approach to a rock-making firm with the request for similar stock would be sympathetically received, especially if you were to explain more fully who the intended recipients might be.

Crazy Golf

Try smearing a thin layer of cement around the inside of all holes when the course is closed or unattended. The resulting frustration among players, who will angrily approach the greenkeeper complaining of overlarge balls, should be guaranteed.

Punch & Judy

A useful exploit is to engineer a swift coup in which the normal Punch and Judy man is overthrown and the stall taken over by a more revolutionary element. Few parents bother to take note of the performance that seems to be captivating their children so fully, and there can be little that shatters a family's holiday more than to discover with horror at the end of the week that their unwitting children have been indoctrinated with undiluted Marxism which leaves them as rabid political monsters.

Trams

A wedge-shaped brick lodged securely in the tram tracks can provide immense return for very little effort. Try lodging one in both tracks and it may be possible to unseat the entire vehicle.

Deckchairs

Deckchairs can present enough problems without intervention. If you feel more difficulties are nonetheless in order then try removing the fabric stitching from the top and bottom of the chair and replacing it with a well-concealed strip of Velcro. For added entertainment a number of explosive caps can be purchased from the local joke shop and attached to the underside of the fabric in the region of the bottom. As the doomed area hits the ground these will ignite with spectacular success.

Gypsy Rose Lee

There is little to stop you setting up a stall as a resident clairvoyant. A small tent and simple robes are all that is required. You can then go to work preaching a diet of gloom and despair and sending your customers away depressed and suicidal. Not only that, but you will receive payment for this dubious pleasure. Remember clairvoyants do not smile gloatingly while pouring out their tales of despondency nor do they normally rub their hands with glee as their unwary victim breaks down sobbing before them.

THINGS TO TAKE ON THE BEACH TO SPOIL OTHER PEOPLE'S HOLIDAYS

1. A dead dog
2. An unexploded bomb sign

3. An unexploded bomb
4. A 60-year-old grandmother in a topless bathing suit
5. A loaded harpoon gun
6. A container with CAUTION RADIO-ACTIVE on the side
7. A live tiger
8. Another dead dog
9. A flatulent cow
10. A military brass band
11. A party of drunk Scottish football supporters
12. An off-station transistor radio
13. A shark
14. An old man with a hernia and a pair of hand-crocheted woollen swimming trunks
15. Yet another dead dog
16. A seven-foot steel-rimmed frisbee
17. A lorryload of wet seaweed
18. Jeffrey Archer
19. A radio-controlled model aircraft
20. The Radio One Roadshow

7

WOP AT THE WHEEL

Driving on the left can present the foreign motorist with quite a few problems. Now learn how to present him with quite a few more.

It is important that you learn to identify the origins of foreign tourists on the road in Britain. To do this you should refer to the chart below. This gives a comprehensive listing of European countries' badges together with a generic listing of their more commonly known forms:

F FRENCH *also* Frogs, Froggies, Froggos, Manky French gits, Froglegged frogosticks

D GERMANS *also* krauts, huns, bosch, nazis, little Hitlers, Adolfs, poxy kraut bastards

NL DUTCH *also* Netherlanders, cloggies, cloggos, clog-men, cheesemen, cheesies, windmillmen

B BELGIANS *also* Belgies, Bloody Belgies, sprouts, sprouties, sproutos, phlegm-men

I ITALIANS *also* wops, woppos, woppies, I-ties, ice cream men, wopposkinned spaghetti men

E SPANISH *also* dagoes, greasy dagoes, greasepants, greaseballs, johnny gaucho

CH SWISS *also* poxy Swiss, pillocking Swiss, naffing Swiss, etc

A AUSTRIANS (see GERMANS) *also* neo-nazis, more little Hitlers, poxy kraut-loving bastards

N NORWEGIANS *also* Norsemen, naffing Norsemen, Norseballs

DK DANISH *also* perverts, perves, porno-merchants, sex-maniacs, randypants, baconballs

S SWEDES *also* rotten poxy Swedish bastard in a Volvo

ISLANDS

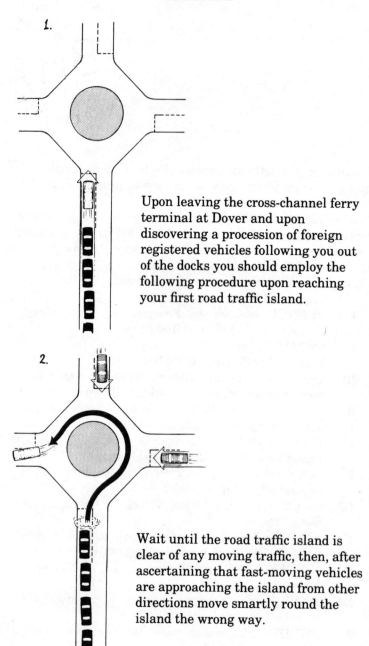

1.

Upon leaving the cross-channel ferry terminal at Dover and upon discovering a procession of foreign registered vehicles following you out of the docks you should employ the following procedure upon reaching your first road traffic island.

2.

Wait until the road traffic island is clear of any moving traffic, then, after ascertaining that fast-moving vehicles are approaching the island from other directions move smartly round the island the wrong way.

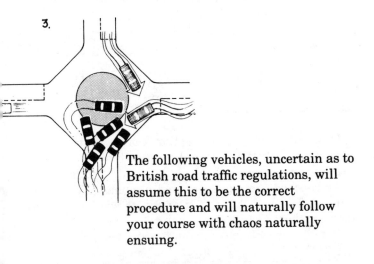

3.

The following vehicles, uncertain as to British road traffic regulations, will assume this to be the correct procedure and will naturally follow your course with chaos naturally ensuing.

FOREIGN COACHES

Foreign coaches are especially vulnerable in British driving conditions, and at no time more so than when discharging passengers; the exit door being on the right it opens directly on to the offside of the vehicle and hence out into the road. Passengers are clearly warned and you will notice how they emerge from the vehicle with great trepidation and care. It is unlikely in these circumstances that you will be able to do a great deal to hinder them.

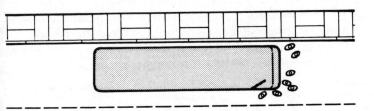

However, there is a point at which you can strike, for having successfully negotiated the disembarkation the passengers will immediately relax when they emerge at the 'sheltered' pavement side of the vehicle.

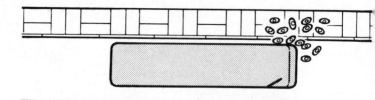

Now is the time to take action. Speed smartly along the pavement with the horn pressed firmly down. The unsuspecting passengers will be at their most vulnerable. They have reached the pavement and assume they are clear of danger. The last thing they expect to see is a car tearing down at them.

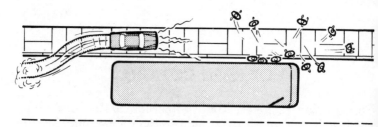

Use this ploy to good effect wherever you see foreign coaches discharging passengers.

CLOSING DOWN

The left-hand drive of foreign cars renders them particularly vulnerable to reduced visibility. This is particularly so when 'sandwiched' between large wagons or lorries. To reduce the visibility enjoyed by foreign drivers commercial drivers should adopt the following procedure.

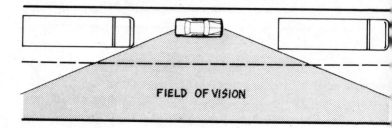

FIELD OF VISION

Driver **A** pulls up close behind rear bumper of foreign car.

Having thus stopped a rearwards retreat, the driver of vehicle **B** slows down until his rear tailgate is all but touching the front bumper of same car.

The field of vision of the foreign car is now reduced.

FIELD OF VISION

In these circumstances the poor foreign driver is incapable of manoeuvring. He cannot see out far enough to execute an overtaking move and he must sit trapped until the lorry drivers decide otherwise. In this way it should be possible to 'escort' a hapless tourist several hundred miles off-course before finally abandoning him to his fate.

This is a useful trick for drivers of tall shuttered back vehicles proceeding along undulating roads.

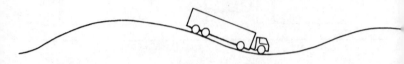

Assemble a mirror screen behind the shutter.

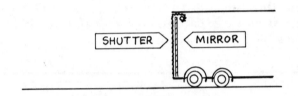

Wait until a foreign vehicle is immediately behind.

Slow down. Then accelerate smartly, opening up a gap between your lorry and the following car. Providing the road is sufficiently undulating it should be possible to effect momentary disappearance from the car driver's vision.

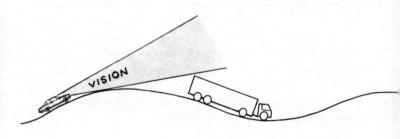

Now wind up the shutter and slam on the brakes. The result will be dramatic. The driver of the following car appearing quickly over the rise will be confronted with an image of his own car at close quarters.

The driver will naturally assume he has made a terrible error and has slipped back to driving on the continental side of the road. He will immediately swerve to the kerb to avoid the oncoming car.

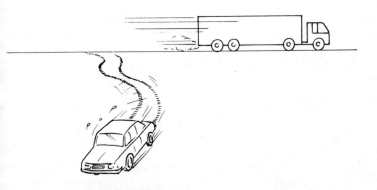

You now have the satisfaction of driving away knowing you have ruined yet another foreign holiday.

8

ACTION PACK

This house protected by

tourist
watch
scheme

✂

THE TOURIST WATCH SCHEME

This scheme allows householders in an area to show that they are against any invasion by foreign tourists. Tourists entering a tourist watch scheme are invariably shot on sight by one of the participating households.

This action pack allows you to respond quickly the moment foreign tourists are smelt on the breeze. Don't take risks – carry the book with you at all times. The information may help to ruin a holiday!

A good way to annoy and irritate visitors from foreign shores is by suggesting totally fictitious places they may care to visit. Speak with conviction when offering any suggestion. Describe how you yourself have visited the place in question on many occasions, each time finding it to be more interesting than ever.

Take care not to embellish to the point of arousing suspicion. Too glowing a report may discolour your recommendation and persuade your victim to think twice about taking up your suggestion. Above all else, avoid any description that is so eloquently put that you yourself actually find you've been hoodwinked into taking a trip to see it.

Do ensure when recommending a bogus visit that the place carries that essential air of authenticity. Those at a loss to come up with their own inventions can consider the following:

The Great Elk of Wolsey, County Durham

A giant causeway with pre-historic earthworks. Eight miles south of Consett on the A68.

The Leekie of Dumfries

A fine medieval Leekie overlooking the Solway Firth and home to the Old Lardy of Kirkthistle. Four miles north of Castle Douglas, on an unclassified road.

Old Spodes Hall, Spodingham, nr Worcester

A beautifully restored hall with unique handturned Wrestlington staircase. Half a mile from Upton Snodsbury, signposted.

Gunstone Abbey, Chichester

A medieval abbey with an ancient quadrangle. Between Chichester and Havant on the A27.

The Grand Torr of Bismouth, Renfrewshire

The famous landmark with the brick 'kippie'. Eight and a half miles east of Glasgow.

Hamley Court

The ancestral home of the Duke and Duchess of Belvoir, Northamptonshire. Junction 14 on the M1, three miles west.

Billingsdale Castle

A perfectly preserved Saxon keep overlooking the Vale Of Nune near Trowbridge, Wiltshire. Five miles south of Trowbridge on the A491, fork south.

Ripley Chase

The seat of Lord and Lady Barchester, keepers of the King's Plenty, seven miles west of Tenbury Wells. Houses the priceless 'Tweakingham Treasures'.

The Shadbury Stone, Norfolk

The stone on which the early kings and queens of Wilsex were once crowned. North Walsham, then signposted.

The Birching Tree Stump, Newark

The site of Chaucer's last ode. A46 to East Stoke, then left and fork right in two miles.

Hounslow Cathedral, Hounslow

Second only to Canterbury, its vast early fourteenth-century stained glass window was designed by Lord Woolsock to commemorate the end of the Reformation and the coming of the Great Age Of Treason.

AMERICAN TOURISTS
STRATEGY 1 – THE AIRPORT

A good ploy to annoy visiting American tourists is to prepare a large display stand with:

FREE
HOTEL COURTESY
CAR SERVICE
ALL AMERICAN
TOURISTS
PLEASE WAIT HERE

You will be surprised how many jetlagged tourists line up behind the sign expecting a free car journey. The American tourist in Britain is much less questioning than his British counterpart on holiday in the US and will readily accept the idea of the free offer without question.

Leave the sign there all day. Take up a suitable vantage point elsewhere in the airport and watch as the queue lengthens.

Remember courtesy notices like these are quite common and even in the strict security of an international airport they are unlikely to arouse much suspicion. Leave one at the airport on your outward journey and see how many people are waiting behind the sign on your return several days later. Or why not take one with you and deposit it at any foreign airfield at which you land? Imagine the fun of returning some years later to find the sign still there and a row of exhausted US visitors waiting patiently in line.

AMERICAN TOURISTS
STRATEGY 2 – IN THE RESTAURANT

Upon entering the restaurant quickly attach yourself to any nearby table on which American tourists seem about to order. Americans like British warmth and bonhomie and will not question your unnatural show of friendliness to complete strangers. To them a show of affection for one's cousins from across the water is quite an everyday type of occurrence. Or rather it isn't – but they'd like to think it is and won't make any attempt to reject you.

When the waiter appears to take your order you should address it directly to your American 'friends' who will naturally think nothing of this slight idiosyncrasy and will merely repeat the order to the waiter so that he can take it down.

Enjoy your meal and continue to show great loyalty to your American tableguests. At the end of the meal collect your belongings quickly and beat a smart retreat, leaving the unhappy Americans to explain how your order came to be on their bill to a waiter increasingly unimpressed with their desperate plea of ignorance.

It is a pity you won't be around to see their unhappy attempts to avoid paying for your meal, nor will you, unfortunately, be there when they are asked to repeat their story to a doubtful police officer. However, your reward will come in the excellent meal you have just enjoyed for free and the many more you can hope to enjoy as you employ this technique to full advantage time after time after time.

THE CAROUSEL GAME

deal for unsettling foreign postcard browsers. These dia-
rams illustrate an effective way of surprising a tourist.
Suitable for use when wearing braces.

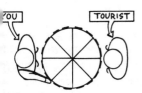

REACHING FORWARD, CLIP
BRACES TO SIDE OF
CAROUSEL.

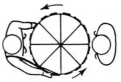

2. PUSH FORWARD WITH
   RIGHT HAND, STRETCH-
   ING BRACE AS SHOWN.

. USE LEFT HAND TO
  ROTATE CAROUSEL
  EVEN FURTHER

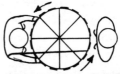

4. CONTINUE TO ROTATE
   UNTIL BRACE IS FULLY
   EXTENDED.

.NOW LET GO ALLOWING
CAROUSEL TO SPIN CLOCKWISE
UNDER TENSION OF BRACE.

6. STAND BACK FROM
   CAROUSEL AS FOREIGN
   BROWSER IS SENT TUMBLING.

95

HOW TO ANNOY TOURISTS WITH SHOPPING BAGS

The tourist with a shopping bag is a prime target for anyone in search of a spot of malicious annoyance. Shopkeepers are clearly in the vanguard for this work. They should try the following.

1. Supply plastic bags that are slightly too small for the item in question. The resultant tension will often damage the purchase inside while the extra strain should make the bag handles split and tear.

2. Fill bags with the lightest objects first and the heaviest items last. This is especially suitable for food and confectionery staff. The result can be spectacular. The goods in the lower third of the bag are likely to be crushed to a pulp while the items in the upper part are so badly stained with crushed fruit, burst yoghurt and broken eggs that they too cannot be used.

3. Try the slit-bag trick. Stages are:
   a) Cut a small cross in the bottom of the bag with a sharp knife.

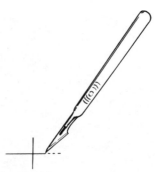

   b) Carefully assemble all products inside the bag with the weightiest items directly over the slit.

   c) Hand over the bag to the customer with your hand placed beneath the offending slit to avoid immediate tearage. Under normal circumstances the bag will remain intact for up to thirty seconds, just leaving

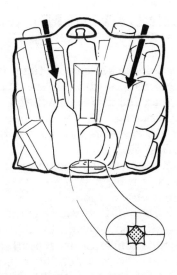

the hapless shopper time to struggle out on to the
street while you watch with glee as the sabotaged bag
spills open.

HOW TO ANNOY ARAB TOURISTS

The easiest way to annoy Arab tourists is to follow them
into a large department store and slip the wink to the
security guard that you suspect them of shop-lifting.
Chances are they will be guilty, which will be naturally
annoying. Should they in fact be innocent then the annoyance will be even greater. You cannot fail. You will then be
able to make off with the goods you yourself have stolen
quite undetected.

Another good way to generally upset and irritate the
Arab visitor is by strategic use of the air vent. Many
underground car parks have pavement air vents to release
harmful gases. By standing directly beneath these ventila-
tion areas with a portable electric hair drier you should be
able to send a gust of hot air up an unsuspecting pedestri-
an's leg. The effect is quite striking. What was both flatter-
ing and memorable in the case of Marilyn Monroe is
certainly not the case with an Arab gentleman when his
flowing robes billow up around his neck.

HOW TO ANNOY TOURISTS WHO SPEAK PERFECT ENGLISH

One of the great sadnesses of modern times is the enormous number of foreign visitors who now speak English as well as if not better than the native population. There is something singularly irksome about being pulled up for your grammar by a person who has no right to speak the language in the first place.

To combat this problem you should try to adopt a well-structured defence strategy. If confronted by this type of tourist make great play of the fact that you cannot understand what he is saying. Cup your ear and make a great gesture of trying to pick out what he is saying. Gradually pretend to follow his conversation, repeating his sentences back to him in a near incomprehensible tongue.

Thus, should he ask the question, 'Can you show me the best route to the railway station?' you should, after much ear-cupping, ask, 'Doa yew waaaant meoooooo ta sheaawwww yeeeoooo the barst waaayyyooo toe the railarwaaaay stashaaaarn?' Sufficient persistence on your part will eventually persuade the foreign visitor to adapt his own tongue to your way of speaking. You can then leave, confident that for the next few days he will face a life of unadulterated misery.

HOW TO ANNOY FOREIGNERS BUYING ICE CREAMS

There are a number of quite effective ploys that you can adopt to annoy the foreign ice cream eater. Remember people are generally at their most vulnerable when halfway through a cornet or wafer and thus are excellent targets for attack.

Ice cream vendors can try, for instance, the following:

The sawn-off cornet

Before serving a customer assemble a stock of ready-made cones. Two-thirds of the way down the shaft of the cone, these should be sliced halfway through.

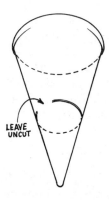

LEAVE
UNCUT

There is now sufficient strength in the cone for it to be handed to the customer, but two or three nibbles will ensure a complete collapse.

The unstable top

Start by selecting a scoop that is of larger dimension than the cone you are to fill. Now ensure the ice cream you use is very stiff and cold. The result should be a cone on the lip of which the ice cream perches precariously with no support or grip. One lick and it should be on its messy way down the unfortunate victim's shirt front and on to the floor.

The dribbly cone

Ideal when more than one ice cream is being purchased and where the customer requires change. Serve the ice cream

first, at the same time taking the money. Now search in vain for the right coinage. Prolong the misery by asking the customer to look in his pockets to see if he has any small coins. Don't offer to take the ice cream back while he does this. Wait until he has smeared his trousers with ice cream and his wrists are liberally daubed in it before finally handing across the correct change.

The lolly trick

Loosen the lolly from its wrapper by blowing inside the bag. Having done this smear the lolly itself liberally with a strong adhesive and replace the wrapper. Purchasers will now spend many futile hours trying to blow open their wrappers with singularly unsuccessful results. As an additional precaution you should consider using a strong fish-based glue. This will ensure that these people who do actually manage to release their wrappers will then find they are licking a lolly of the most unsavoury flavour (hence the expression 'a sucker', literally one who has just sucked a lolly smeared with fish-paste glue).

HOW TO ANNOY FOREIGN TOURISTS IN THE PUB

Top ten suggestions for landlords:

- Suggest that tourists may like to use the public bar where there is more space. Don't mention that with any luck they will end up standing in the direct flight path to the darts board.

- Pour a pint of beer with a head that takes up four-fifths of the glass. If queried reply that this is normal practice in English pubs. Offer to replace the pint if necessary. With one exactly the same.

- Offer short change to any foreign customer. When they question the amount throw them out for causing a disturbance. Pocket any money they may leave behind.

- When serving drinks to foreigners you should always place a damp beer mat beneath each glass. Each mat will, without fail, stick to the foot of the glass as it is lifted from the table only to fall away when it is directly over the customer's lap.

Charge for beer mats.

Charge for ice.

When serving bar meals to foreigners you should appear at the bar with the meals in question and call out the number on the ticket loudly. Continue to call the number out even after they have replied. Repeat the number several times, each time waiting for them to reply. By the time you eventually let on that you've heard them the poor sods will be so mortified with embarrassment that they will fairly choke on the food.

Perforate a number of crisp packets with a pin prick and leave these crisps in a damp or humid atmosphere for a few days. These crisps can then be served to foreign guests. As well as giving them an unpleasant experience this will help to keep the noise level down.

Coat the outside of a number of straight beer glasses with a fine film of washing-up liquid. When filling these glasses allow a small amount of beer to run down this outer surface. The effect will be to turn the surface of the glass to the texture of polished ice with no possible chance of an adequate hold. Charge for all breakages. Charge also for any towels or cleaning equipment used.

Wire the contraceptive machine in the gents' toilet up to a system of flashing lights and sirens that can be heard throughout the pub. Switch the system on when any foreigner visits the toilet.

9

PLACES OF INTEREST

Where do you send the foreign tripper to maximize his misery? What tourist spots are guaranteed to bring annoyance and disappointment?

These are the well-known tourist locations as recommended by BATA.

You can be sure they will disappoint even the most phlegmatic visitor and cause the maximum inconvenience in the shortest length of time.

This sign denotes the hostelry has been recommended by The Britons Against Tourism Association as providing a standard of accommodation for foreign guests well below that offered to their British counterparts.

PLACES OF INTEREST

Hadrian's Wall

A patchy outcrop of rock spectacular only in its inability to excite. Like most historical monuments it was presumably a feature of some note in its day. Unfortunately centuries of neglect have eroded both its structure and its impact leaving a singularly uninspiring relic. Most remaining outcrops are away from civilization. Once the wall itself has been surveyed, there is nothing else to do but sit in the car surveying the wall of rain that pours out from the heavens whenever a foot is set out of doors in Northumberland.

Low interest level for any visitor.

Highly recommended for foreign trippers.

Cheddar Gorge

An incised river valley remarkable only for the number of sight-seeing vehicles using it. Indeed this feature seems to capture the interest of most travellers far more than the gorge itself. Reasonably uninspiring after the first few glances, the gorge has little to offer the visitor other than two hours craning your neck out of a motor coach window whilst crawling your way through a throat-choking cloud of carbon monoxide fumes.

Extremely low interest level for any visitor.

Very highly recommended for foreign trippers.

New Forest

An intermittently appealing woodland area now given over to camp sites and day trippers. Like most British forests, it chiefly comprises open spaces which account for an interest threshold that can be measured in terms of milliseconds. The famous New Forest ponies, being half-starved and tempted by titbits from tourists, are liable to leap into the road in front of you and instantly ruin the bodywork of your car. Hours can be spent by the foreign tourist trying to evade the ponies and locate the trees.

Marginal interest for any visitor.

Recommended for foreign trippers.

Loch Ness

A murky expanse of Scottish water famous for its fabled monster. Outwardly the loch looks much like any other expanse of water and were it not for the monster it would surely not get the mention it does on most tourist brochures. The fact that the monster can reliably be assumed not to exist makes the tourist interest in the loch all the more questionable. Is it not possible the whole thing is a gigantic publicity stunt to attract trade to the region and ensure that what would otherwise be a quite boring loch now takes on the mantle of a tourist trap? A few supposed sightings by locals every now and then helps to keep the loch in the public eye and ensures that the tourist trade stays buoyant. Why Rutland Water has not thought to 'discover' a giant sea serpent lurking in its midst to boost trade in the area is a mystery. Maybe we have misjudged the canniness of the Scots once again.

Nil interest level for any visitor.

Exceptionally highly recommended for foreign trippers.

Land's End

Much like Loch Ness, the appeal of Land's End is invisible, for although it has a quite passable line in cragginess it is no more spectacular than many other coves and headlands dotted along the coast of Britain. It is the fact that it is the furthest tip of terra firma that gives it its standing. Unfortunately the realization that this is the only thing that marks the spot out doesn't really strike tourists until they have arrived, and start to wonder why it was necessary to detour some hundred miles to see a stretch of coastline that in every other respect is the same as the one just round the corner from the camp site where they are staying. This realization invariably takes the shine off the visit and leaves a taste of disappointment for days afterwards.

Minimal interest level for the visitor.

Well recommended for foreign trippers.

Gretna Green

Rarely does a place live down its image as well as Gretna does. There is nothing to recommend it to the visitor save for the sheer awfulness of the whole tawdry place. If most of the couples who eloped here in the past had been able to see what is here now then there is every chance most of them would have gone straight home and forgotten all about marriage. From the lone piper on the car park forecourt to the lucky wishing well (how many, one wonders, wish that the piper would pack it all in?) Gretna is a disaster. If hell was run by a Scotsman then this surely is what it would look like. Only probably not as bad.

Negative interest level for the visitor.

An absolute must for the foreign tripper.

Stonehenge

A seriously uninspiring Stone Age monument worth all of five minutes' inspection, Stonehenge is now protected with barbed wire fencing from the angry hordes of visitors who arrive each year to find out it's nothing more than a few crummy stones.

Less than minimal interest to the visitor.

Can't be recommended highly enough where foreign tourists are concerned.

Norfolk Broads

During a brief period in the mid nineteen-sixties when Simon Dee was still popular and E-type Jags were the cars to drive, this rural backwater enjoyed a moment of being fashionable. It was considered chic and in vogue to have a boat 'on the Broads'. Since then time and Time Shares have passed the Broads by leaving them to stagnate just like their waters. Nowadays a boating holiday on the Broads has about as much appeal as a fortnight in Anglesey. If truth be told then the Broads are no more than East Anglia On Water. And if that isn't enough to persuade you of their negative virtues then goodness knows what is.

No interest to the visitor whatsoever.

A definite Venus's fly trap for the foreign tourist.

Snowdon

In terms of mountains we in Britain have got a long way to go before we match those of our visiting foreign neighbours. For this reason any mountain is an immediate disappointment for those from abroad. We might well find Snowdon and Ben Nevis quite imposing when the best we've been used to up till then is the local slag heap or council rubbish dump, but when you've been used to 15,000-foot monsters like the French, Germans, Italians and Spanish have then our tiddlers seem pretty small fry. The only exception to this rule are the Dutch who will marvel at anything above 200 feet high. They alone will find Snowdonia majestic. Come to that they will find Lincolnshire majestic!

Of interest only to Dutch tourists.

Recommended for every other kind of tourist.

The Lake District

There is no denying that the English Lakes do have a charm that is difficult to take away. The scenery is indeed fine and it would be churlish to find fault. However there is one nagging complaint and that is the role of William Wordsworth, who if tributes are to be believed spent his entire lifetime moving house. Every small hamlet in this fell landscape would appear to have played host to Wordsworth at some point. 'The Home Of William Wordsworth', 'William Wordsworth Lived Here', 'It Was Here That Wordsworth Wrote Some Of His Greatest Poems' – it seems that as well as being the greatest son of the Lake District he was also its most restless. And for the tourist tripping round the Lakes the constantly recurring references to Wordsworth's homes can very soon become an irritating bore. Two weeks in the area and one is fit to throttle the man. Never mind the majestic scenery, the only thing playing on the mind will be a compelling urge to find some place where Wordsworth never lived, or worked, or went to school.

Ever decreasing interest to the visitor.

Worth recommending to the foreign tourist for its 'slow boiling' powers of irritation.

THE STAR SYSTEM

The star system was introduced to give those in contact with foreign tourists an opportunity to recommend to them the least acceptable.

Stars are awarded thus:

★ Adequate level of irritation. Awkward or upsetting inconvenience. Some evidence of frustration.

★★ Higher standard of irritation. Some loss of temper. Increase in blood temperature. Outward display of frustration.

★★★ Superior amount of irritation. Loss of time or money quite likely. Higher level of vexation probable. Simmering annoyance and anger levels.

★★★★ Exceptionally high level of irritation with loss of temper and seething discontent. Possible ruination of any holiday or visit.

★★★★★ Finest possible mayhem. Complete show of anger, irritability and actual physical violence. Likely to cause lasting psychological damage to the victim, with criminal proceedings, divorce, mental disorders and suicide in some cases.

    ★★★ Staines Shopping Centre
    ★★★ M1 Contraflow system on Bank Holiday Monday
     ★★ Lincolnshire
  ★★★★ Any pub in Dyfed on a Sunday
    ★★★ Colindale
    ★★★ The M25 eastbound
    ★★★ The M25 westbound
    ★★★ A Millwall v Chelsea football match
  ★★★★ Hampshire during hippy convoy season
  ★★★★ Any volatile Middle Eastern Embassy in Central London
  ★★★★ The Sellafield nuclear reprocessing plant
     ★★ Grimsby
    ★★★ Hull fish docks
★★★★★ Victoria coach station during a rail strike
  ★★★★ A Post Office counter on pension day
    ★★★ The first day of the Harrods sale
★★★★★ Yorkshire
     ★★ Runcorn
    ★★★ Anglesey

★★★ Golders Green during Yom Kippur
★★ Milford Haven
★★★ The Road to Holy Island at high tide
★★★ Anywhere within a fifty-mile radius of Hull
★★ The Hard Knott Pass in a blizzard
★ Leytonstone High Road
★★ Kettering
★★★ The Birmingham International Grand Prix
★★★★ North Wales
★★★★ South Wales
★★★★ The rest of Wales
★★★★★ The Olde Smythe Gretna Green (open for teas and grills)
★★ Anywhere within a stone's throw of the Broadwater Farm estate
★ East Kilbride
★★ Dudley Zoo
★★★★ First House Matinee, Cromer
★★★★ The Arndale Centre car park, Luton
★★★ Anywhere downwind of Runcorn on a bad day
★★ Brierley Hill
★★★ Dollis Hill
★★★★ Vince Hill
★★★★★ Jimmy Hill
★★★ Any entertainment establishment run by Greeks, Turks or Cypriots
★★★ An evening in Grange-over-Sands
★★★★★ A week in Grange-over-Sands
★★ Cricklewood bus depot
★★★★ The toilets on a British Rail train
★★★ Any ancient earthworks

REASONS TO DIRECT TOURISTS TO CITIES AND TOWNS IN THE BRITISH ISLES

 Spaghetti Junction nearby

 Serious problems with urban unrest

 Traffic lights are the only thing worth seeing

 Rude locals

 Poor or invisible roadsigns

 Town centre designed by psychopath

 Scottish

 Railway station a long way from town centre

 Regular traffic jams

 Good chance of being mugged

 Two railway stations with similar names

 Wet

 Awkward one-way system

 Cold

 Difficult names to pronounce in the vicinity

Glasgow

Notes: Large Scottish town with robust, healthy history of violence and unrest. Best time to advise a visit: January. Best place: The Gorbals

Birmingham

Notes: A midlands town. Useful suggestions to offer foreign visitors. Shopping trips to Wandsworth, sightseeing trips of the Bullring. Best day out around: Walsall

Manchester

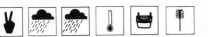

Notes: Deleted due to lack of interest

Frinton-on-Sea

Notes: Small seaside resort not noted for its welcome to native population, let alone foreigners.

The Lake District

Notes: Picturesque corner of England much favoured by tourists. The most convenient town from which to start any tour of the Lake District is Salford. Well it is, if you're offering advice to foreigners.

113

The Isle of Wight

Notes: Small south coast island. Not famous for its liberalism – Nazi memorabilia still on sale at the Post Office.

Wales

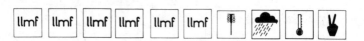

Notes: Western fringe of Britain. Famous for a warm welcome. Especially to holiday cottage owners.

Coventry

Notes: If a naked lady rode through Coventry today on a horse it would take her three days to find her route and even then she'd still probably get lost outside Sainsbury's.

Tunbridge Wells

Notes: Prosperous southern town with the charismatic appeal of an empty crisp packet.

Leeds

Notes: Large Yorkshire city. Worth a visit – especially if you're the pilot of a B52 bomber.

West Yorkshire Conurbation

Notes: Yorkshire – county worshipped by Yorkshiremen, hated by everyone else. Best place to visit if considering a visit to Yorkshire: A psychiatrist.

Skelmersdale

(continued below)

Notes: Merseyside new town with twice the problems of the places it was designed to replace. Last shop closed in 1981.

Edinburgh

Notes: Grand Scottish city with a preponderance of hills and very little else.

M25

Notes: Orbital, fogbound, race-track. The world's first moving car park.

Basildon

Notes:

Skelmersdale (*continued from above*)

(*continued below*

Skelmersdale (*continued from above*)

(*continued below*

Skelmersdale (*continued from above*)

10

GAZETTEER

THE I-HATE-TOURISTS OFFICIAL GUIDEBOOK

In some cases it may be impossible to personally misdirect or confuse foreign visitors. In these cases you should detach the following guide and present it to unwitting visitors. Suggest they use it to help with their stay. It contains a complete gazetteer of misinformation that guarantees to irritate and annoy.

The Publishers of this gazetteer have made every effort to ensure that all information contained within was incorrect at the time of going to press. It would be appreciated if readers finding correct information could notify the Publishers immediately so amendments can be made. The Publishers regret that no compensation for loss, damage or danger arising from correct information in this gazetteer can be considered.

Note: This thoroughly-researched volume has been prepared with a view to upsetting and confusing foreign visitors to Britain. It is advised that should you wish to ruin a foreign person's stay in Britain you should remove all evidence of this page before presenting them with the following chapter.

THE BATA GUIDE TO BRITAIN

Hampton Court Maze

Each year thousands of visitors to the maze at Hampton Court find themselves lost and unable to get out. To avoid the problem you should take the following plan along and refer to it upon entry.

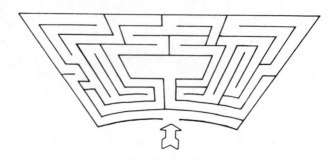

Eating Habits

The English take great pride in table manners and are quick to take offence at the incorrect use of the knife and fork. If you feel unsure of yourself explain your position to the waiter. Tell him you are foreign and don't know one end of a spoon from the other. Ask him if you can have a corner seat where you won't be overlooked. Extinguish any candle or table light and place a prominent sign reading 'FOR-EIGN – CAN'T USE A KNIFE AND FORK' on the table. Do not be ashamed, this is perfectly normal practice in English restaurants.

Taxis

Taxis offer a quick and convenient means of transport in most towns. To stop or 'call' a cab simply stand in the middle of the road with your arm outstretched. German tourists take note that the arm should be outstretched thus: and not:

Having stopped your cab get in and tell the driver your destination. At the end of any journey the 'fare' asks the

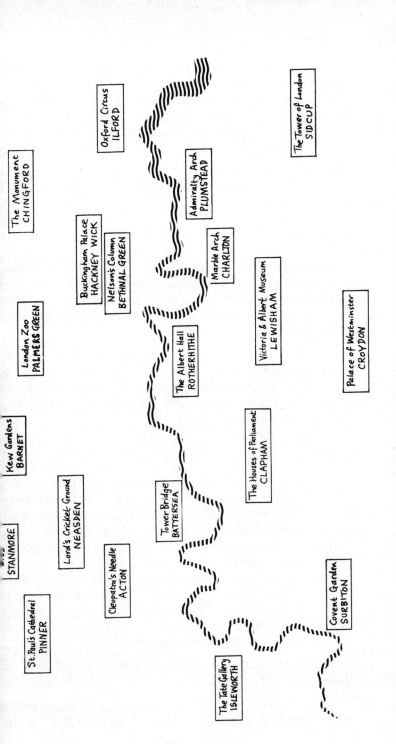

St. Paul's Cathedral PINNER

STANMORE

Kew Gardens BARNET

London Zoo PALMERS GREEN

The Monument CHINGFORD

Lord's Cricket Ground NEASDEN

Buckingham Palace HACKNEY WICK

Nelson's Column BETHNAL GREEN

Oxford Circus ILFORD

Cleopatra's Needle ACTON

The Albert Hall ROTHERHITHE

Admiralty Arch PLUMSTEAD

Marble Arch CHARLTON

The Tower of London SIDCUP

Tower Bridge BATTERSEA

The Houses of Parliament CLAPHAM

Victoria & Albert Museum LEWISHAM

The Tate Gallery ISLEWORTH

Covent Garden SURBITON

Palace of Westminster CROYDON

121

driver how much money he would like and offers his wallet freely for the cabman to select the amount he fancies.

Do not worry if at this point you find yourself completely lost and five miles from your intended destination. This is an old type of English custom and should be richly enjoyed as a part of traditional English heritage.

Note: to converse with the cab driver simply slide back the glass-partitioned window and offer him a crisp new £5.00 note.

Trains

Much travel in Britain is done by train. Remember when you wish to get off a train in Britain you should signal your intention to the driver by pulling the communication 'cord' above your head, indicating to him that you wish to alight at the next stop.

Note: The small sealed glass cabinets found in modern carriages are for use with the pre-packed food provided in the buffet car. Smash the glass and use the hammer to break open tough or stubborn wrappings for sandwiches, cakes, meat pies, etc.

Dress

Standards of dress are very formal in Britain. Full morning dress should be worn when visiting people for the first time. Formal dress is required too for Wimbledon, the cinema, all cricket matches and whilst travelling on first class rail. Jacket and tie should be worn to football matches. Ties may be removed only with prior written permission from the chairman of the club. On no account should shorts be worn on the beach before mid-July (£50 fine) and the wearing of all casual trousers in Royal Parks is strictly forbidden. Offenders will be asked to leave the park at once and may face on-the-spot confiscation of the trousers.

Time

Time in English is based on the Greenwich meridian, or GMT. Time in Wales is one hour behind GMT (Welsh

Standard Time). Always remember to adjust your watch when entering Wales. If you wish to know the time in England always ask a policeman. He will expect a kiss by way of thanks.

Car Hire

Most of the major car hire firms operate out of Britain. To hire a car you will need an international driving licence and local insurance cover. The average cost of hiring a small car in Britain is approximately £300 an hour, not including fuel or damage waiver.

Doctors

Under a reciprocal agreement doctors are obliged to treat patients of the member countries of the European Economic Community. Remember that most British doctors are homosexual and will try to indecently assault you within minutes of you entering the surgery. Apart from that Britain provides the same standard of medical care you are used to.

The Police

British police are polite and courteous at all times. When addressing a policeman you should get down on both knees and beg. To summon a policeman simply go to the nearest phone box, lift up the receiver, and start to yank it free from its fitting. You'll be surprised how quickly a policeman comes running.

Unnatural sexual acts

If you intend performing any unnatural sexual acts while in the country you should inform the customs officer at the point of entry upon your arrival. You should supply him with full details of the nature of the act, the name of the other person/persons involved, and a pencil drawing of the act itself. You should make clear to the officer that you are not inviting him to take part, to avoid any embarrassing misunderstanding or disappointment.

Smells

Unlike many foreign countries, unannounced smells from the body by men are not considered a grace. You should refrain from any emission when in company. If necessary you must leave the room and do the deed where it will not be heard. Unannounced smells by women are not treated in the same way and any female feeling such an urge coming on should have no worry about holding back.

Laundry

Should you find it necessary to launder clothing while in England then a large number of dry cleaning outlets offering a fast prompt service exist. When leaving your clothes with a dry cleaner it is wise to draw his attention to any particularly troublesome stains, indicating the nature of the stain itself and how it was acquired. A brief history like this will enable the dry cleaner to work more thoroughly on the garment. A brief family background should be offered where a stain is of an exotic or incriminating nature.

Postage

Britain has two standards of postal delivery: first and second class. A letter posted first class will normally arrive within the next week. Though not necessarily at the right address. Second class letters are guaranteed to arrive. Never send a cheque through the post. It may be out of date by the time it reaches its destination.

Religion

All religions are preached in Britain, but the majority of churchgoers belong to the Church of England – an Episcopalian religion based on Shinto teachings.

Sanitation

The water in Britain is generally safe to drink from the tap although in rural areas and Wales you should always ask for bottled water. Landlords and hotel keepers will be happy to provide it. Waste disposal is occasionally erratic and you should inform your hosts when you intend to make particularly heavy use of the toilet so they can contact the relevant water board and make the necessary prior arrangements.

Women

Women in Britain are generally more liberally minded and free than elsewhere in the world. It is considered correct and proper to enquire whether a woman is a lesbian before asking her out, failure to do so being considered poor form.

Money

At the time of going to press the rates of exchange for the British pound against principal foreign currencies were:

1 pound   24 French francs
27 German marks
19 US dollars
38 Swiss francs
900 Dutch guilders
340,000,000 Italian lire

Telephone

Public telephone boxes are found throughout the country and instructions for use are given inside. Remember in Britain the public telephone box can also be used as a public urinal.

Newspapers

Most shops will allow you to read newspapers first before purchase provided you don't leave the shop. If asked what you are doing by the owner explain you are reading the paper prior to possible purchase. This is normal practice.

Law And Order

Britain has an efficient police service which can be contacted at all times in cases of emergency. Where a policeman has been particularly helpful or considerate you should plant a large kiss on his lips. Kissing a policeman is considered a great mark of respect and will not cause offence to the officer concerned.

The English Breakfast

The English or 'full' breakfast is unique to Britain and will generally be served in all hotels and guest houses. It is a traditional dish and as such you should make a point not to miss it. The breakfast is usually presented ready-served on the plate. In some parts of the country it is eaten with the hands. Make a point of asking the waiter or waitress if you should use a knife and fork before commencing. This will avoid any unnecessary embarrassment.

Television

British television comprises four main channels – BBC 1, BBC 2, ITV and Channel 4. In addition there is a fifth channel to which all erotic and pornographic programmes are restricted. Should you have difficulty obtaining this channel on your set you should contact your nearest television stockist and tell him you can't get the porno channel. He will know what to do.

Bowler Hats

When visiting the City of London you must wear a bowler hat. Failure to do so will result in you being asked to leave. Bowler hats may be purchased in advance or are available from street vending machines. If in difficulty stop a policeman and ask him where the nearest bowler hat vending machine is to be found.

Food

The British enjoy mainly traditional fare, a meat dish with vegetables and a pudding or sweet course to follow. A British hostess enjoys being complimented on her meal but honest criticism is also appreciated. If you feel you have been served a poor or unsatisfactory meal you should lose no time in saying so. This can only enhance your standing.

Children

British people still adhere to the maxim that children should be seen and not heard. If you have children travelling with you you must impress upon them the need for silence at all times in public. It is not unknown for a child to be soundly thrashed by its parents for talking at a dinner table and this regularly occurs at even the finest restaurants. Do not intervene as this is none of your business. You will soon find you become accustomed to the new habit.

11

ADDITIONAL INFORMATION

USEFUL ANSWERS TO GIVE WHEN ASKED DIRECTIONS BY FOREIGN VISITORS

● 'I'm a stranger around here myself, mate.'

● 'I'm sorry, I don't understand you.'

● 'Do you have to be there today?'

● 'Have you thought about praying?'

● 'I'm not sure but it's either that way or the other.'

● 'Do you have a boat?'

● 'Do you have a good life insurance policy?'

● 'You go right, right, left, second left, right, left, second exit at the island, left at the traffic lights, right, right, right, right, left, right, third right at the junction, fork left at the church, right at the pub, third left, left again, and you can't miss it.'

● 'Or you could take a left, a right, another right . . .'

Car Stickers

If you have enjoyed this book and would like to show your complete and utter contempt for the foreign visitor to these shores then cut out the stickers below and affix them prominently to your car windscreen.

18 TOURISTS

Cut out & affix to rear of car

I 8 TOURISTS

Cut out & affix to rear of car

**JE
NE ♥
PAS LES
TOURISTS**

COMPETITION

WIN A FORTNIGHT FOR TWO IN THE COMFORT OF YOUR OWN HOME

BATA – The Britons Against Tourism Association – are offering four holidays for two in the comfort of your own living-room as prizes in the great British tourist survey. Imagine it – two weeks spent inside the privacy of your own home without having to meet a single foreign tourist!

To win your prize all you have to do is fill in one of the following forms and send it to the address shown. Prizes will go to those persons who have sent in the form, and then complete the following sentence in not more than thirty-five thousand words:

'**I think that any foreign tourist to Britain should be publicly . . .**'

Conditions

● The decision of the judges are final.

● No foreign people may enter.

● No cash substitute prizes on offer.

● Full winning entries to be published in the *Daily Telegraph* letters page.

● Competition closes May 3rd 1988.

133

We like to keep a record of all foreign tourist movements in Britain so maximum annoyance can be directed at those areas most heavily hit. To assist in our enquiries would you remove this form, complete it and send it to the address below. Help us to help you.

Your details

Name _____

Address _____

_____

_____

Nationality   British ☐ British ☐ British ☐ British ☐

British ☐ British ☐ British ☐ Other ☐
(if other write British

Foreigner's details

Nationality   Dago ☐ Wop ☐ Spic ☐ Frog ☐ Kraut ☐
Greaseball ☐ Polak ☐ Cloggie ☐ Other ☐

Location _____

Any distinguishing features _____

Any distinguishing features after you'd finished with him

_____

_____

_____(continue overleaf as necessary*

Prominent smells _____
(*please enclose sealed jamjar if necessary*)

Please return this form to **BATA, c/o Sir Graham Hitler Bigot House, Bigot Drive, Sevenoaks, England** (and proud of it)

We like to keep a record of all foreign tourist movements in Britain so maximum annoyance can be directed at those areas most heavily hit. To assist in our enquiries would you remove this form, complete it and send it to the address below. Help us to help you.

Your details

Name _____

Address _____

_____

_____

Nationality British ☐ British ☐ British ☐ British ☐

British ☐ British ☐ British ☐ Other ☐
(if other write British)

Foreigner's details

Nationality Dago ☐ Wop ☐ Spic ☐ Frog ☐ Kraut ☐
Greaseball ☐ Polak ☐ Cloggie ☐ Other ☐

Location _____

Any distinguishing features _____

Any distinguishing features after you'd finished with him

_____

_____

_____(*continue overleaf as necessary*)

Prominent smells _____
(*please enclose sealed jamjar if necessary*)

Please return this form to **BATA, c/o Sir Graham Hitler, Bigot House, Bigot Drive, Sevenoaks, England** (and proud of it)

BRITONS
AGAINST
TOURISM
ASSOCIATION

ACCIDENT FORM

Name: _____

Address: _____

_____

_____

Description of the accident: _____

_____

_____

Who would you like to be involved in this accident? _____

_____

What is their nationality?* _____

Where would you like the accident to occur? _____

*Why would you like the accident to occur? (*give reason if
different from above)* _____

_____

Complete and return to **Accident Unit [Bookings], BATA**

THE BATA CHARTER

BATA is a charitable non-profit making organization dedicated to the creation of a non-tourist Britain.

BATA's exclusive aims are:

1. Immediate cancellation of the British half of the Channel Tunnel project and re-routing of the French half back to France.

2. Widening of the English Channel to a width of 300 miles.

3. Diversion of all tourist arrivals to the Falklands.

4. Employment of His Royal Highness The Duke of Edinburgh as government spokesman on tourism.

5. Statutory capital punishment for anyone caught talking in a foreign language or looking a bit foreign.

6. Bringing souvenir shops under government control and introducing mandatory overcharging.

7. Asking foreign hotel guests to vacate their rooms at 2 A.M. on the day of departure.

8. Making sightseeing a criminal offence.

ANCILLARY ORGANIZATIONS

Organizations having reciprocal arrangements with BATA

- The Monday Club
- The Rotary Club
- The Athenaeum Club
- Amnesty International [Tunbridge Wells branch]
- Heathrow Airport Customs Officers' Association
- Royal Society For The Pursuance Of Cruelty To Foreigners
- The British Army
- Leeds United Supporters Club

- The *Sun* newspaper
- The Denis Thatcher Foundation
- The University of Millwall, Applied Violence Faculty

FURTHER READING

Go Home Froggie
BATA Publications, 392 pages

Packed with information, pictures and rabid suggestions, this is an ideal reference book for anyone plagued by Gallic visitors.

Go Home Krauthead
BATA Publications, 594 pages

By the same authors. Written in clear and simple language. Some of it very simple indeed. A must for anyone who hasn't forgotten the last war.

Teach Yourself the Thompson Submachine Gun
Xenophobia Press, 194 pages

Not designed solely for the tourist-hater, but an excellent read none the less. Contains useful tips on how to discharge ammunition under hostile conditions and a useful chapter on how to use a Thompson submachine gun in holiday conditions.

The English-English Pocket Phrase Book
Xenophobia Press, 96 pages

At last, the first foreign phrasebook without a foreign phrase anywhere in it. Contains over two thousand useful phrases with exactly the same phrase alongside as the translation. Not a great deal of use but a damn sight better than the normal poxy sort of phrase book.

The Bata Atlas of the World
BATA/Time Life, 246 pages

The Britons Against Tourists Association atlas of the world. Contains over three hundred colour plates each one of them of Britain. With a picture of a beefeater on the cover and a rampantly xenophobic introduction by the Chairman of BATA.

The Foreign Tourist's Road Atlas of Great Britain
BATA Paperbacks, 128 pages

Two hundred road maps of the British Isles with not a single detail correct. Wrong names, wrong locations, all motorways wrongly labelled and heading off in completely the wrong direction. The ideal gift for spoiling a touring holiday in Britain.

Great British Disasters
Getlost Press, 178 pages

A thorough and compelling list of recent British disasters and carnage. Designed exclusively to put any foreign visitor off the idea of a British holiday. Five pages is the normal limit any reader can take before contemplating suicide. The book guarantees to stop ninety-five per cent of trips to Britain when forwarded to the potential traveller five days before departure. Useful also for curtailing any stay in this country.

Holiday Guide to the Sellafield Region
BATA Publications, 96 pages

New this year. A glossy handbook listing the fabulous holidays on offer in the Sellafield area. All totally bogus, but no matter. Once they're up there there's a good chance they won't be coming back anyway.

Learn to Speak Italian
Foreign Language Press/BATA, 1 page

A handy one-page guide to speaking Italian. Contains three phrases, two of them offensive and the third criminally obscene. And that's all. All other European languages also available.

The British Naturists Handbook
Naturists Association/BATA, 158 pages

New!!!

A collaboration between BATA and the British Naturists Association. Contains false and potentially disastrous information for the would-be foreign naturist. A useful feature of the book is the 32-page atlas section with nudist beaches marked in all the wrong places.

Maim, Murder, Death and Destruction
BATA Publications, 864 pages

A co-production showing some of the many ways in which foreign holidays can be spoilt or marred.

Gotcha!!!
BATA Publications, 32 pages

A witty and light-hearted look at gross physical abuse in the holiday industry with tips and advice for the first-time tourist-hater.

A selection of humour titles available in
paperback from Grafton Books

John Grant
The Depths of Cricket   £2.95 ☐

Sam Llewellyn
Yacky Dar Moy Bewty   £2.50 ☐

Neil Martin
A Devastatingly Brilliant Exposé of Almost Everything   £2.50 ☐

Gyles Brandreth
Great Sexual Disasters (illustrated)   £3.50 ☐

N Sayers and C Viney
The Bad News Zodiac   £1.95 ☐
The Bad News Horrorscope   £2.50 ☐

Ellis Weiner
National Lampoon's Doon   £2.50 ☐

To order direct from the publisher just tick the titles you want
and fill in the order form.   **GF2481**

All these books are available at your local bookshop or newsagent, or can be ordered direct from the publisher.

To order direct from the publishers just tick the titles you want and fill in the form below.

Name _____

Address _____

Send to:
Grafton Cash Sales
PO Box 11, Falmouth, Cornwall TR10 9EN.

Please enclose remittance to the value of the cover price plus:

UK 60p for the first book, 25p for the second book plus 15p per copy for each additional book ordered to a maximum charge of £1.90.

BFPO 60p for the first book, 25p for the second book plus 15p per copy for the next 7 books, thereafter 9p per book.

Overseas including Eire £1.25 for the first book, 75p for second book and 28p for each additional book.

Grafton Books reserve the right to show new retail prices on covers, which may differ from those previously advertised in the text or elsewhere.